NEW DIRECTIONS
FOR TEACHING AND
LEARNING

Number 3 • 1980

NEW DIRECTIONS FOR TEACHING AND LEARNING

A Quarterly Sourcebook
Kenneth E. Eble and John Noonan, Editors-in-Chief

Number 3, 1980

Fostering Critical Thinking

Robert E. Young
Guest Editor

Jossey-Bass Inc., Publishers
San Francisco • Washington • London

FOSTERING CRITICAL THINKING
New Directions for Teaching and Learning
Number 3, 1980
Robert E. Young, Guest Editor

New Directions for Teaching and Learning is published quarterly by Jossey-Bass Inc., Publishers. Subscriptions are available at the regular rate for institutions, libraries, and agencies of $30 for one year. Individuals may subscribe at the special professional rate of $18 for one year.

Correspondence:
Subscriptions, single-issue orders, change of address notices, undelivered copies, and other correspondence should be sent to *New Directions* Subscriptions, Jossey-Bass Inc., Publishers, 433 California Street, San Francisco, California 94104.

Editorial correspondence should be sent to the Editors-in-Chief, Kenneth E. Eble or John Noonan, Department of English, University of Utah, Salt Lake City, Utah 84112.

Library of Congress Catalogue Card Number LC 80-80836

Cover design by Willi Baum

Manufactured in the United States of America

Contents

Editor's Notes: Critical Thinking— A Renewed Interest

Midcentury was a time of great optimism about the contributions of higher education to American democracy. Colleges and universities, and we as teachers in them, were challenged to train students for citizenship as well as for work. The key ingredient in this training, it seemed, was the "ability to think critically." The curriculum included courses across the disciplines, which attempted to teach this ability. Words like these were not uncommon: "The good life in a democratic society . . . seems to rest fundamentally on one's ability to think critically about the problems with which he is confronted. The essence of the creed is that each person possesses potentialities for discovering his own problems and for developing personally satisfying and socially acceptable solutions to them, so that he has no need to defer completely to the will of authority . . . ." (Dressel and Mayhew, 1954, p. 35). Both liberal and professional education, at least in principle, set their sights on these potentialities.

In the last quarter of the century, things seem less simple and less optimistic. Democracy itself seems a less secure ideal, and we have again become self-conscious about our ability to *think critically.* Vietnam, Watergate, Three Mile Island, and Iran, along with double-digit inflation and energy cost increases have caused us to question our competence as a people to solve the problems and make the judgments that affect our ways of life. Though blame has yet to be placed foursquare on the colleges and universities, their role in promoting not only knowledge itself but the ability to put it to use has been cause for renewed concern. This volume is a testimony to that concern.

The decade-long decline in test scores (College Entrance Examination Board, 1977; Myers, 1979), the continuing debate over the relationship between education and work ("Education and Work . . . ," 1979; Vermilye, 1977) and the new movement in general education (Carnegie Foundation for the Advancement of Teaching, 1977; "Project on General Education Models," 1979) have all raised provocative questions about what we have done and what we should do in postsecondary education. Although these issues have catalyzed different groups and different responses, each seems to rest on a common observation: a great many students enter and leave our colleges and universities without basic skills, without basic understandings, and without ways of thinking that are not limited to a specialized area. Social imperatives and national priorities have liberalized the curriculum and placed the emphasis on its vocational aspect. The result has been an "academic downgrading of those aspects of an undergraduate [and graduate and professional] education that encourage imagination, judgment, decision, and values" (Rudolph, 1977, pp. 287-288).

From these issues and others, hope for the democratic ideal and higher education have reemerged. However, the tone now is more critical and urgent. As one writer puts it, "It is not fair to ask educators to do the basic job of institutional overhaul, but it is fair to expect [education] to equip Americans with critical faculties needed to make sound choices and also to be aware that in a democratic society the society is theirs to shape, not be shaped by it" (Raskin, 1979, p. 24). And in the view of another, "education is a process of teaching people to think and allowing them to come to their own conclusions. Presumably that is the fundamental task of the university's program . . . but it is a task the universities often fall short of performing" (Gomberg, 1979, p. 32). The authors of the chapters in this volume wish to contribute to this reemergence and the task of "teaching people to think."

Whether education is for democracy or for work, the job rests with teachers and students. Both groups need to bring special resources and expend special energies. The rewards for a job well done are considerable, not only for the society as a whole but for each individual teacher and student as well. But the job is not without difficulty. Though it is both a democratic ideal and a future social imperative, there is resistance to teaching for critical thinking in many quarters. In Chapter One, Kinney observes that "students and teachers alike are pained, and in analogous ways, by the problems of critical thinking—who needs it, can it be taught, can it be learned?" (p. 4). This volume explores these questions and others important to students, teachers, and those who support them.

Critical Thinking: What Is It?

Philosophers, psychologists, and educators all have laid claim to the concept of critical thinking. Each group has different purposes and approaches, but each group helps us to be more concrete in our thinking about our attempts to foster it.

Socrates' dictum, the unexamined life is not worth living, reflects a readiness to question assumptions, which is essential to critical thinking, and both Plato's emphasis on rational analysis and Aristotle's empiricism provide important foundations for the concept of critical thought. Modern philosophers have concerned themselves with identifying the methods, such as comparison, classification, inference, and deduction, that allow us to solve the abstract and practical problems of life. In an up-to-date fashion, critical thinking has become the "use of intelligence in making decisions" (Organ, 1965). Teaching critical thinking in courses in logic and practical reasoning involves instructing students in those methods and that use of intelligence.

Psychologists emphasize cognitive structure and activities of the mind. For example, Jean Piaget (1972) suggests that a small number of primary structures (that is, whole/part, classification/hierarchy, cause/effect, and sequence) form the basis of any activity of mind, while Guilford (1967) relates thinking to 120 separate intellectual operations which the organism performs when processing information. Critical thinking can be characterized by the ways in which the contents and mechanisms of human cognition are involved in the solution of problems and the making of decisions and judgments. Teaching is concerned with the development of these contents and mechanisms.

Educators have focused on the objectives of formal education. Though necessarily attentive to cognition and philosophical methods, those most concerned with curricula, teaching methods, and assessment of students have tried to define the goals of education in the realm of critical thinking and to develop ways of achieving these goals. A number of taxonomies of objectives has been fashioned. Bloom and his associates (1956) proposed that students be assessed for their knowledge, comprehension, analysis, synthesis, and evaluation related to any content area. Though each of these things, with the exception of knowledge, can be thought of as "thinking," it is *evaluation* that characterizes critical thought, since it engages all the other abilities. The definitions of Bloom and others have helped teachers and students to focus instruction and to communicate its intents. Perry (1970) has evolved an equally provocative and useful scheme. He suggests that students move through a series of steps in the evaluation of people, knowledge, and values, in which their thinking becomes less simple, categorical, and absolute. Curricula and teaching methods aim to foster this development toward its appropriate end, truly critical thought and action.

For higher education, the work of the Cooperative Study of Evaluation in General Education put critical thinking into focus as an objective of teaching and learning. Although the concept does not embrace all thinking, and although it is not clear or acceptable to everyone, "As a starting point . . . it perhaps can be accepted that students—as one result of their educational experience—should be able to carry on types of mental activity more complicated than simple recall and restatement of ideas, facts, principles, etc., given in the textbook or presented by the instructor in his lectures" (Dressel and Mayhew, 1954, pp. 176–177). These types of mental activity were summarized (by the educators who worked on the study) into five skills of critical thinking (Dressel and Mayhew, 1954, pp. 179–180):

1. The ability to define a problem
2. The ability to select pertinent information for the solution of the problem
3. The ability to recognize stated and unstated assumptions
4. The ability to formulate and select relevant and promising hypotheses
5. The ability to draw conclusions validly and to judge the validity of inferences

Dressel and Mayhew propose that critical thinking can serve as a principle for integrating the curriculum as "a point of view towards problems and their solutions and a way of thinking about basic problems faced by mankind" (p. 273). Their approach is a good starting point for this volume. Each of the following chapters grapples with the meaning of critical thinking for teaching. Each chapter reflects philosophical, psychological, and educational approaches and purposes. Each chapter suggests objectives, activities of mind, and methods which define attempts to foster critical thought. Yinger specifically and systematically distinguishes this kind of thinking from other educational outcomes. He describes those factors—the student's knowledge, intellectual skills, attitudes, and the learning environment—which, taken together, influence the attempts of teachers and students to achieve the goal of critical thinking.

Critical Thinking: Can It Be Taught?

It is one thing to define critical thinking and another to teach it. Faculty dining room debate finds that some instructors think that critical thinking can be taught and that others are far less sanguine. Those who think that it cannot be taught either point to factors resistant to college-level instruction—inheritance or earlier schooling—or suggest that thinking is simply the result of the thorough mastery of content. However, recent research and instructional development suggest that the intellectual operations which define critical thinking can be developed by exposure to a college curriculum and elicited through teaching strategies and certain kinds of practice (Bloom, 1953; Dressel and Mayhew, 1954; Fuller, 1977; Furedy and Furedy, 1979; Glaser, 1941; Kerr, 1978; O'Brien and Shapiro, 1973; Perry, 1970; Smith, 1977).

Studies that measure the effects of college have consistently found increases in intellectual aptitude, intellectual achievement, and the ability to think critically (Feldman and Newcomb, 1969). Most recently, Whitla (1978) found that the ability to present organized, logical, and forceful arguments increased dramatically among students of five four- and two-year colleges in New England. Using the Whimbey method, John U. Monro reports marked improvement at Miles College and Tougaloo College in students' abilities to perform mental tasks ordinarily associated with intelligence. Teachers in a variety of disciplines have successfully used a number of different approaches to help students enhance their ability to think critically (Logan, 1976; Lyle, 1958; Zaccaria, 1978).

A major obstacle to the teaching of critical thinking has been the lack of useful models and strategies for colleges and classroom teachers to use in developing intellectual operations. Twenty-five years ago, Dressel and Mayhew hoped that learning theories would come to have more direct applicability to the teaching situation, that critical thinking itself would be viewed in less limited and compartmentalized ways, and that objectives for critical thinking would be integrated into existing curricula and courses, rather than merely tacked onto them. To an important degree, these hopes have been realized. Although few courses are explicitly designed to encourage critical thinking, models and strategies to assist colleges and teachers in fostering it are emerging. In addition to the examples cited above and the current work in general education ("Project on General Education Models," 1979), schooling at the lower levels, as well as business and industry, can contribute useful ideas and approaches (Davis, 1973; Kuo, 1976). The chapters in this volume present other promising strategies and examples. Stonewater describes and analyzes four approaches to the teaching of problem solving, approaches designed by teachers which have been used successfully in a range of disciplines and with a variety of students. Svinicki and Kraemer study one attempt to teach critical thinking to large numbers of students. They help us understand the joys and pains which teachers and students encounter in this enterprise.

Critical Thinking: Can It Be Evaluated?

This question may be the most straightforward of all, but it may also be the most difficult to answer. Recently, an experienced professor asked this question on a final exam: "One of the purposes in this course has been to give you experience in rational, critical, and analytical thinking in connection with the investigation of historical materials. Have you found stimulus in this regard? If you have, discuss your experience and give specific examples."

This question figured in a series of more typical questions that required the critical thinking the professor had hoped to foster. He asked the question not to avoid the difficulty of crafting another question to measure critical thinking but because he knew instinctively that, although the products of critical thinking are relatively easy to assess, the experience of it usually eludes both the teacher and the student. *How* it happens is as interesting and important as *whether* it does. Insight into students' thinking can suggest pathways to understanding that a teacher can travel again with other students. It also provides an opportunity to correct the thinking before students judge that it is accurate and put it into use. For students, the opportunity to articulate the process of their thought can help them to understand when they succeed and when they fail, and it also provides a guide to future thinking.

The final chapter in this volume deals directly with the assessment of critical thinking. But each chapter provides some direction to testing as it describes and illustrates the products and processes of critical thinking.

All the chapters in this volume were written with one assumption in mind: to know more about critical thinking—what it is, what influences it, what works and what does not in teaching and testing it—will be helpful to college and university teachers. The authors have not attempted to develop a cookbook, although they all have tried to present ideas that professors and those who support them can use in thinking about and planning for the teaching of critical thinking. Individually, the authors have different perspectives and have written in different styles. But all have set out to add knowledge, insight, and interest to work on this important education goal.

Robert E. Young
Guest Editor

References

Bloom, B. S. "Thought Processes in College Students." *Journal of General Education,* 1953, *7,* 160-169.

Bloom, B. S. (Ed.). *Taxonomy of Educational Objectives: Cognitive Domain.* New York: McKay, 1956.

The Carnegie Foundation for the Advancement of Teaching. *Missions of the College Curriculum: A Contemporary Review with Suggestions.* San Francisco: Jossey-Bass, 1977.

College Entrance Examination Board. *On Further Examination: Report of the Advisory Panel on the Scholastic Aptitude Test Score Decline.* New York: College Entrance Examination Board, 1977.

Davis, G. A. *Psychology of Problem Solving: Theory and Practice.* New York: Basic Books, 1973.

Dressel, P. L., and Mayhew, L. B. *General Education: Explorations in Evaluation.* Washington, D.C.: American Council on Education, 1954.

"Education and Work: Two Worlds or One." *Change: The Magazine of Learning,* 1979, *11* (5), 1-57.

Feldman, K. A., and Newcomb, T. M. *The Impact of College on Students.* San Francisco: Jossey-Bass, 1969.

Fuller, R. G. (Ed.). *Multidisciplinary Piagetian-Based Programs for College Freshmen.* Lincoln: University of Nebraska Press, 1977.

Furedy, J. J., and Furedy, C. "Course Design for Critical Thinking." *Improving College and University Teaching,* 1979, *27* (3), 99-101.

Glaser, E. *An Experiment in the Development of Critical Thinking.* New York: Teachers College Press, Columbia University, 1941.

Gomberg, W. "Education and Leisure: New Curricula." *Change: The Magazine of Learning,* 1979, *11* (5), 30-34.

Guilford, J. P. *The Nature of Human Intelligence.* New York: McGraw-Hill, 1967.

Kerr, O. H. "Critical Thinking and Teaching Excellence." In *Papers of the Fourth International Conference on Improving University Teaching* (Aachen, Germany, July 26-29, 1978). College Park: University College, University of Maryland, 1978.

Kuo, Y. Y. *Teaching Strategies for Developing Intellectual Abilities.* Muncie, Ind.: The East-West Cultural Exchange, 1976.

Logan, C. H. "Do Sociologists Teach Students to Think More Critically?" *Teaching Sociology,* 1976, *4,* 25-48.

Lyle, E. "An Exploration in the Teaching of Critical Thinking in General Psychology." *Journal of Educational Research,* 1958, *52,* 129-133.

Myers, C. "Verbal, Math SAT Scores Decline to All-Time Low." *The Chronicle of Higher Education,* September 17, 1979, p. 6.

O'Brien, T. C., and Shapiro, B. J. "Logical Thinking in College Students." *Educational Studies in Mathematics,* 1973, *5,* 71-79.

Organ, T. W. *The Art of Critical Thinking.* Boston: Houghton Mifflin, 1965.

Perry, W. G., Jr. *Forms of Intellectual and Ethical Development in the College Years.* New York: Holt, Rinehart and Winston, 1970.

Piaget, J. "Intellectual Evolution from Adolescence to Adulthood." *Human Development,* 1972, *15,* 1-12.

"Project on General Education Models." *GEM Newsletter,* No. 1. Washington, D.C.: Project on General Education Models, 1979.

Raskin, A. H. "The Shape of Work to Come: Perils." *Change: The Magazine of Learning,* 1979, *11* (5), 21-24.

Rudolph, F. *Curriculum: A History of the American Undergraduate Course of Study Since 1636.* San Francisco: Jossey-Bass, 1977.

Smith, D. G. "College Classroom Interactions and Critical Thinking." *Journal of Educational Psychology,* 1977, *69* (2), 180-190.

Vermilye, D. W. (Ed.). *Relating Work and Education: Current Issues in Higher Education 1977.* San Francisco: Jossey-Bass, 1977.

Whitla, D. K. *Value Added: Measuring the Impact of Undergraduate Education.* Cambridge, Mass.: Office of Instructional Research and Evaluation, Harvard University, 1978.

Zaccaria, M. A. "The Development of Historical Thinking." *History Teacher,* 1978, *11,* 326.

Robert E. Young, formerly associate director of the Center for Improving Teaching Effectiveness, is now director of the Office of Instructional Development at the University of North Dakota. He is interested in the thinking activities of both students and teachers in higher education. The incentive and idea for this book grew out of work with faculty members as they try to foster critical thinking among an increasingly diverse student body.

Critical thinking has a special value to the society, yet employment and teaching practices emphasize learning of other sorts. Students resist critical thinking in the curriculum, maybe for good reason.

Why Bother? The Importance of Critical Thinking

James J. Kinney

Before the turbulent sixties, we assumed that students in college learned how to think. Now we are not so sure. Beginning in the early sixties, as the open-door community college exploded on the academic scene, hundreds of thousands of "new students" poured into higher education, bringing with their typically authoritarian personalities a dogged suspicion of intellectual pursuits (see, for example, Cross, 1971). At the same time, among traditional students, some frog-eyed dopers, their brains fried by LSD, ran wild, screaming obscenities and systematically trashing the life of the mind.

The seventies brought a retreat from the barricades, but they also saw the appearance of such less-than-critical goings-on as TM, est, Rolfing, and Hare Krishnas and Moonies in the airports. Today's generation of students seems to have retreated into fantasy games of "Dungeons and Dragons," science fiction, materialistic selfishness, and deliberately chosen, technically-limited curricula. Now people both in as well as out of the academy are concerned.

The Call to Critical Thinking

It does not require much documentation to establish that critical thinking is an important commodity in a highly sophisticated technical society. While assembly-line work may remain mindlessly repetitious, research and development, procurement, product supervision, and marketing—activities for which the college-educated are traditionally recruited—require well-developed analytical and critical skills. A study of the nation's 7,500 largest companies ("Survey Finds Major Educational Effort Operated by Firms," 1977) found employers most concerned about employees' lack of skills in thinking and communicating. Too many supervisors, managers, scientists, and other professionals are unable to organize and present their ideas to others. The cry for critical thinking can be heard in academe as well. Most professors whom I know claim that their primary concern is to teach students how to think. Intellectual rigor, excellence, and critical thinking have become cant terms in the aftermath of the sixties. And administrators and classroom instructors have become draftees in the battle against the "new primitivism," as Yale's A. Bartlett Giamatti (1976, p. 19) characterizes the attitudes and involvements of students in the aftermath of the sixties and the seventies.

A sense of conflict prevails when institutions and faculties are dedicated to the teaching of critical skills that students stubbornly resist. Why do students resist their professors' call to critical thinking, which society seems to support? Authoritarian personalities and mindless solipsism may afford partial explanations. It is possible also that students are exercising more critical acumen than we give them credit for. The call to critical thought is often heavily qualified. Students are often aware of this fact.

As at most institutions, our university placement service issues a bulletin listing employers who will be interviewing on campus. The current bulletin lists ten organizations. Five of the ten will see liberal arts graduates, whose majors have honed their analytical skills during four long years. Five out of ten sounds pretty good until you notice that four of the five are insurance companies in search of "marketing representative trainees" and that the fifth is a shoe company which specifies that candidates will begin as shoe salespersons. The other five organizations—banks, government agencies, and a major industrial firm—are interviewing only candidates expecting degrees in business administration, computer science, economics, information systems, mathematics, physics, and psychology. Thus while professors call for critical thinking at a broad, conceptual level, society buys analytical skills that are narrow, technically-grounded, and algorithmic. Student preference for training rather than education simply reflects the marketplace.

None of this is news. It is common and comfortable for academics to blame a philistine society when their students ignore or resist pleas to think critically. However, as the comic strip character Pogo once remarked, the enemy may well be us. Professors say that their main concern is to teach students how to think, but textbooks, course outlines, assignments, and tests often reflect a greater concern for covering neatly packaged material in ways that avoid critical issues in the respective disciplines and that encourage analysis only in tightly defined contexts.

My own discipline, English, has long prided itself on developing the analytical, synthetic, and evaluative skills associated with criticism—skills at the top of Bloom's taxonomy. Almost universally, students are introduced to this discipline through freshman composition. However, at the majority of colleges and universities, freshman composition is still concerned with topic sentences, paragraphs, outlines, and correctness (Tigar, 1974). Richard Ohmann argues (1976) that, at the very best, such courses can only turn out writers capable of producing the Pentagon Papers; that is, of cogently organizing, clarifying, comparing, and contrasting available options without once ever examining their context or challenging their premises. Even in literature courses, a strongly algorithmic approach predominates. The New Criticism, which originated in the 1920s, offers a formulaic approach to critical analysis. A story, for example, is broken down into the "elements of fiction"—plot, character, setting, point of view, theme, imagery, symbolism—and each element is examined to see how it interacts with the others to generate an acceptable "reading" of the story, one that ignores the context in which the story was written, and the context in which the student lives, in order to stress the "universal" values. This suggests that, even for a discipline that is centered on "critical thinking," the constraints on that activity are more numerous than we like to think.

Students' and Teachers' Response

What are the implications of this ambivalence about critical thinking for teachers and students? Student indifference to the call seems one obvious result. Students today make judgments more experientially than conceptually. They live in a network of working fathers, mothers, older brothers and sisters, friends, and relatives. Career choices are made not so much from a general socially approved concept of altruistic work but from media reports about teachers who drive taxicabs, about social workers crushed by caseloads, and physicians and lawyers making good money. Students hear that business leaders insist that communications skills are vital, but they see that the same businesspeople hire accountants and hope that they can write, not that they hire English majors and hope that the latter will learn some accounting on the job.

The conflicts between the stated importance of critical thought and the reality of higher educational institutions today—whether large university or small community college—are all too apparent. Liberal arts courses are no longer at the center of the institution, and what they teach is perceived tangential to the work going on in the colleges of business, agriculture, engineering, medicine, and law or in the career-education technical programs. Today's students have never known colleges and universities to be different. It is hardly surprising, then, that many students shrug off background chatter about critical thinking as not only irrelevant but alien. Their job, they feel, is to get the training necessary for entry into a promising career, not to waste time learning how to think critically in order to become a shoe salesman.

Generalizations are risky, and all students do not fit this pattern. But a recent survey by the *Chronicle of Higher Education* ("Fact File," 1980) clearly shows that students are migrating away from disciplines traditionally associated with the development of critical thinking to the advantage of business, technical, and medical fields. The problem is not that students have clearly defined career goals that determine their choice of programs but that students assume that their choice negates the need to concern themselves with such apparently peripheral values as critical thinking. This assumption is visible in many ways, not the least of which is students' disregard for what they might learn from a course in favor of single-minded concentration on a good grade.

In response, many teachers adopt an approach that is not dissimilar from that in which masses of students doggedly go through the motions while their real interests lie elsewhere. Tenure, promotion, and professional recognition come to those who devote their energies to research and publication, not to challenging seemingly inarticulate and uninterested students to think critically.

In short, students and teachers alike are pained, and in analogous ways, by the problems of critical thinking—who needs it, can it be taught, can it be learned? Many students are convinced that they need only specific technical training to get by in the world. Some teachers are convinced that students cannot think, while many question whether students can learn to. So why bother?

The Case for Critical Thinking?

A good focal point for an examination of the problem can be found in freshman composition courses. Traditionally, a major charge for these courses has been to teach students to think critically. Typical composition texts have for years contained sections on argument, which catalog the ways of inductive and deductive reasoning, the use of evidence, and logical fallacies. Further, freshman composition very often includes an introduction to literature; that is, to the methods of analyzing short stories, poems, and plays in order to write critical essays about them. During the past decade, however, the emphasis has been shifted to the process of writing itself, with increased attention being paid to "invention" procedures used to generate ideas at the beginning of the writing process. Increasingly, writing is considered to be a way of thinking (Elbow, 1973; Emig, 1977), and writing teachers have devoted time and energy to grappling with the cognitive processes involved.

Because traditional drill in logical induction and deduction seems ineffective with today's students, teachers have turned for assistance to cognitive scientists. In the last five years, most issues of *College Composition and Communication,* the principal journal in the field, have read like paeans to a holy trinity composed of Vygotsky, Piaget, and Bruner. This resort has been helpful and reassuring to many in the field, but it raises as many questions as it answers, especially about what we mean by critical thinking and what are the possibilities for fostering it.

Rather uncritically, some writing teachers have accepted the position that thinking is problem solving. Many new textbooks include a set of procedures to use and questions to raise whenever a "problem" rears its head—a sort of all-purpose toolkit for thought. But the view of thinking as problem solving is modeled on computer programming, on the simple encoding of information. As Berthoff (1972) has powerfully argued, this view seems to deny the symbolic complexity and generative power of language and human thought. Critical thinking is better considered an expanding, exploratory process than the progressively narrowing process of problem solving.

Another response to the problem of definition has been to equate critical thinking with Piaget's level of cognitive development called *formal operations*—that is, the ability to abstract, analyze, and synthesize and to form true concepts and manipulate them symbolically. Unfortunately, this definition quickly leads to the conclusion that many college-aged students have not developed cognitively beyond a stage of thinking that in Piaget's scheme is characteristic of much younger children. For example, Lunsford (1979, p. 41) states flatly that "most of our basic writing students are operating well below the formal operations or true concept-formation stage of cognitive development, and hence they have great difficulty in . . . performing tasks which require analysis and synthesis."

However, it has been argued that this is simply not true. Labov's (1970) proof that dialect differences do not prevent the full development of conceptual processes set the stage for this argument. Cole (1978, p. 58) asserts that adults who have never been exposed to education are capable of performing analytical mental operations. The effect of education, he says, is not to develop basic cognitive abilities but only to transmit "specific skills required to process arbitrary information under constrained conditions using literate devices." Donaldson (1979) directly challenges Piaget's idea that the inability to "de-center"—that is, to focus equal attention on a variety of factors or to get outside one's own perspective—lies at the base of the inability to perform experimental tasks at the level of formal operations. Donaldson concludes that children as young as three years old are quite capable of de-centering, but that at any age they have difficulty performing mental operations of which they are otherwise capable if the task is "disembedded" from any meaningful human context. Children and adolescents can analyze, synthesize, and form concepts, but not under circumstances where the context is so artificial that there is no meaningful human reason for performing these operations. This echoes Cole's position on education, and it suggests that, while college students can in fact de-center and think analytically, they may still have great difficulty doing so in the disembedded context of classes and assignments.

Disembedded thinking is highly valued in the marketplace, where engineers and advertisers are required to use their analytical skills to design and sell products, not to consider the full context of their human, social, and ecological cost. Disembedded thinking is also valuable in many classrooms, if not most, where the problems posed are abstract and removed from the everyday contexts that facilitate thought. Though a case can and should be made for the teaching and learning of what we have called disembedded thought, I wish to suggest that critical thinking should mean more than this. If it does mean more than this, then it should be worth bothering about.

Educating for Critical Thinking

Society seems to demand that people should be educated in the ways of critical thought, and higher education seems resolved to do the job, but there is no simple answer to the question of how this best can be done. One key to the answer lies in recognition of the complex links between cognition and context. Ong (1971, 1977) argues persuasively that thinking differs in oral and literate cultures and that the skills which we generally associate with critical thinking are possible only among literate people. Increasingly, however, students come from what Ong describes as a culture based in "secondary orality." Moreover, the current literature on brain hemisphericity suggests that cultural background influences the mode of cognition, propositional or appositional, that will predominate in any one individual (Roueche and others, 1979). Bernstein's work in the sociology of language (1974) indicates that the difference between children of high and low socioeconomic status lies not so much in their ability to think but in the form that their language takes when encoding thought, with children of low socioeconomic status relying on a context-heavy "restricted" code, while children of high socioeconomic status learn to use a relatively context-independent "elaborated" code. Thus educators need to consider students' linguistic and cultural contexts when attempting to teach new ways of thinking. Recognition that students have learned to think in contexts that make immediate human sense to them seems to be the necessary first step in any attempt to teach the skills of analytical thought in situations disembedded from such contexts.

Many teachers have begun to focus on the problem of context in one way or another. Certainly, the increased use of simulation, games, role-playing, case studies, and internships are all evidence of a growing resolve to create some intermediate stage between the context of the student's immediate life and broader, more distant contexts. Some writing teachers of late have focused attention on the problem of audience. They give assignments that simulate actual writing situations encountered in work or other circumstances. Some teachers of literature, influenced by the recent Copernican Revolution in literary criticism, have abandoned the New Critical approach, which demands immediate confrontation with disembedded analysis, for an approach that uses the context of the student's life and the context of the class itself to evolve or negotiate an interpretation of a literary work. These attempts recognize that students are distanced from disembedded thinking and that the way to that goal lies through stages, but even these attempts do not guarantee that thinking skills learned in intermediate contexts can be transferred to distant and unfamiliar contexts.

Two approaches to the problem of transfer of thinking skills come to mind, one pedagogical, the other structural. Pedagogically, it would seem worthwhile to address the problems of context directly in class. Teachers should spend time explaining the problem and devise teaching strategies that do not allow students to think that they are being asked to perform outside of a meaningful context but place them at the center of expanding concentric circles. Teachers should not ask students to disembed right away. Students should be helped to see themselves and their work as firmly implanted in a series of ever-broadening contexts.

Almost any area of the curriculum provides a good setting for this kind of progression. Students could be asked to research something in terms of their immediate needs. For example, they could be asked to define the combination of stereo components that would be the best buy for them (a classic example of problem solving). Next, they could investigate the research, design, production, and marketing decisions involved in putting such equipment on the market. Beyond that lie larger considerations of the economic, social, and cultural impact of mass-marketed audio equipment. Only in the last fifty years has human history known a world filled with reproduced sound. As a result, values have been affected by song lyrics, rock stars have become culture heroes, and lifestyles have been built around discos and huge legitimate and illegitimate industries. The concerns are endless, but even as the questions, research, and analysis become increasingly abstract and analytical and less experiential, there is a meaningful context at every level which grows out of and surrounds what comes before. In a manner quite opposed to that of typical problem solving, students would expand their concerns until they reached a level of truly critical thought, where they began to understand that not all problems have solutions and that not all questions have answers. They might even reach that stage beyond critical thinking described by the poet Rilke (1954, p. 35): "Be patient toward all that is unsolved in your heart and try to love the questions themselves like locked rooms and like books that are written in a very foreign tongue. Do not seek the answers, which cannot be given you because you would not be able to live with them. And the point is, to live everything. Live the questions now. Perhaps you will then gradually, without noticing it, live along some distant day into the answer."

The structural approach requires a rethinking of the organization traditional in higher education. Usually the curriculum has tried to build a broad base of general education and foster critical skills for later application in some specialized field. For example, lower-division writing and humanities requirements have been a base for upper-division training in such majors as business and education, and a liberal arts undergraduate major has been viewed as preparation for postgraduate training at a professional school. However, many undergraduates today seem to resent these requirements and view them as unrelated to preparing them for the world of work. In marked contrast, returnees to education in their thirties and forties show a burning interest in precisely those writing and thinking skills scorned by their eighteen-year-old classmates (Kinney, 1979). Thomas Cottle (1980, p. 89) quotes one thirty-year-old woman who gave up a job as a well-paid administrative assistant to enroll in college full-time: "There's a much more important difference between the rest of the students and me. We don't agree at all on what it means to be a success. They think in terms of money, material things. I suppose that's normal. They don't understand that with a nice home, and decent job prospects, and two beautiful children, I know I am a failure . . . I'm a failure until I have knowledge, until I can work with it, be excited by and play with ideas. I don't go to school for rewards down the line. I want to reach the point where I don't measure knowledge by anything but itself."

"Knowledge measured only by itself" comes close to what many consider to be the best feature of disembedded, critical thinking. Maybe we should save education in critical thinking for those who value it enough to seek it out, or at least for those who have satiated their need for job training. We could invert the present undergraduate setup and place the broadening general education requirements designed to foster critical thinking in the last year or two instead of the first. More radically, we could eliminate education for critical thinking from the undergraduate curriculum, reserving it to graduate school. Given the state of things today, this is something we might at least think about—critically, of course.

References

Bernstein, B. *Class, Codes, and Control: Theoretical Studies Towards a Sociology of Language.* London: Routledge & Kegan Paul, 1974.

Berthoff, A. E. "From Problem-Solving to a Theory of Imagination." *College English,* 1972, *33* (6), 636-649.

Cole, M. "How Education Affects the Mind." *Human Nature,* 1978, *1* (4), 50-58.

Cottle, T. J. "Life Studies: Overcoming an Invisible Handicap." *Psychology Today,* 1980, *13* (8), 89.

Cross, K. P. *Beyond the Open Door: New Students to Higher Education.* San Francisco: Jossey-Bass, 1971.

Donaldson, M. *Children's Minds.* New York: Norton, 1979.

Elbow, P. *Writing Without Teachers.* New York: Oxford University Press, 1973.

Emig, J. "Writing as a Mode of Learning." *College Composition and Communication,* 1977, *28* (2), 122-128.

"Fact File." *Chronicle of Higher Education,* January 28, 1980, pp. 4-5.

Giamatti, A. B. "Sentimentality." *Yale Alumni Magazine,* January, 1976, pp. 17-19.

Kinney, J. "Lack of Basic Skills Among Community College Students Causes Alarm." *Humanities Report,* 1979, *1* (9), 9-14.

Labov, W. "The Logic of Non-Standard English." In F. Williams (Ed.), *Language and Poverty.* Chicago: Markham, 1970.

Lunsford, A. A. "Cognitive Development and the Basic Writer." *College English,* 1979, *41* (1), 38-46.

Ohmann, R. *English in America: A Radical View of the Profession.* New York: Oxford University Press, 1976.

Ong, W. J. *Rhetoric, Romance, and Technology.* Ithaca, N.Y.: Cornell University Press, 1971.

Ong, W. J. *Interfaces of the Word.* Ithaca, N.Y.: Cornell University Press, 1977.

Rilke, R. M. *Letters to a Young Poet.* (Trans. by M. D. Herter Norton.) (rev. ed.) New York: Norton, 1954.

Roueche, S. D., and others. "Cognition and Context: Concerns for the Culturally Different Student." *Community College Review,* 1979, *7* (1), 16-25.

"Survey Finds Major Educational Effort Operated by Firms." *Higher Education and National Affairs,* 1977, *26* (23), 7.

Tigar, P. "ADE Survey of Freshman English." *ADE Bulletin,* 1974, *43,* 13-23.

James A. Kinney, assistant professor of English at Virginia Commonwealth University, has been a community college teacher and administrator, a visiting professor at the University of Florida, and a National Endowment for the Humanities fellow at the University of Massachusetts. He is currently engaged in studies in rhetoric and in the preparation of community college English teachers.

The author takes critical thinking apart piece by piece to help teachers understand how it works and how to affect it.

Can We Really Teach Them to Think?

Robert J. Yinger

When discussion among educators turns to such topics as critical thinking, creative thinking, problem solving, and decision making, the question posed by my title frequently arises. This question expresses the very real tension between hope and skepticism that prevails in the minds of many teachers. The knowledge and skills related to critical and other kinds of thinking are important goals for the college and university curriculum. Therein lies the hope expressed by an affirmative answer to the question. Yet many teachers doubt the possibility of affecting, much less of teaching, such complex and elusive skills as those associated with thinking. Can we really teach students to think?

This volume focuses on critical thinking and how to foster it. I will emphasize the psychological issues related to teaching critical thinking. When we ask the question, "Can we teach . . . and if so, how?", there are two types of information that should help: increasing evidence from research on teaching and learning, and psychological studies of thinking processes. These lines of inquiry suggest the important variables that affect thinking during instruction. I will describe these variables and give examples of the insight into critical thinking which they provide.

The Concept of Critical Thinking

How we teach largely depends on how we view the teaching/learning process. For this reason, the concepts and categories that are appropriate for looking at critical thinking should be valuable when we think about teaching it.

Critical thinking has come to mean several very different things. The lack of a clear definition has not, however, prevented educators from regarding critical thinking as a worthy educational goal, nor has it prevented researchers from studying critical thinking or from developing methods for teaching it. Nevertheless, the problem remains: What is critical thinking? Can we "unpack" this well-worn concept to discover its essential elements?

Definitions of critical thinking can be grouped into two categories. Some educators and researchers have employed a broad definition, viewing critical thinking as synonymous with other general thinking processes. Dewey (1933), for instance, equates critical thinking with reflective thinking, and Aylesworth and Reagan (1969) associate it closely with problem solving. More frequently, however, critical thinking has been defined narrowly. One of the most common definitions of critical thinking was proposed by Ennis (1962): "the correct (or reasonable) assessment of statements." Judging the adequacy of arguments supporting a resumption of the draft, identifying Rousseau's assumptions about the nature of man, and analyzing the impact on physics of the publication of Galileo's *Two New Sciences* are instances of critical thinking tasks as Ennis defines them. Many other definitions follow in the same line, all of them focused on the evaluation of the products of thought.

The more popular, narrow definitions of critical thinking reflect the tendency of most educators (and of psychologists also) to view critical thinking as a self-contained "type" of thinking like creative thinking or problem solving or decision making. This perspective emphasizes the differences among intellectual activities at the expense of the important similarities and commonalities to be found among them. I suggest that critical thinking is an essential element of all these intellectual activities. To explain, let us take a look at the basic aspects of thought.

Aspects of Thought. Thinking activity has two basic aspects: the creative and the critical. The creative aspect allows us to generate new ideas, possibilities, and options. The critical aspect allows us to try out, test, and evaluate these products. All complex thinking activity involves both aspects, though possibly in varying mixtures.

The types of mental activities that have typically been regarded as creative or productive are the generation of ideas (whether completely new or information reproduced from memory), the elaboration of information or ideas, the transformation of information in thought, and the combination or recombination of thought contents. All of these processes are directed toward formulation of information previously not available for use by the individual or others. In contrast, critical thought involves such mental activities as the recognition of information (including understanding and comprehension), the testing and verification of ideas and information, and the judging of thought products. These evaluative activities focus on the manipulation of products generated by previous thinking efforts (either one's own or others').

Another approach to the simultaneous presence of creative and critical aspects in thinking is to examine the stages or steps that have been attributed to various types of thinking. The steps involved in four models of complex intellectual activities—problem solving, decision making, creative production, and invention—are compared in Table 1. When the steps in these models are aligned in parallel columns, the similarities among these activities become obvious. It also becomes clear that all four activities involve both the creative/productive aspects and the critical/evaluative aspects of thought. (Steps that primarily involve critical/evaluative thought are printed in italics.) The alternation between the creative and critical aspects is apparent in all four models, though it is especially salient in Rossman's (1931). Although theorists often represent activities in a linear manner, they acknowledge that in practice these activities involve many instances of backtracking to previous steps. In other words, the interaction between the creative and the critical seems to be a very common characteristic of complex thought. This interaction may also be the essential characteristic of thought in general. Miller, Galanter, and Pribram (1960) proposed

Table 1. Four Models of Complex Intellectual Activities

Problem Solving (Dewey, 1933)	*Decision Making (Simon, 1976; Janis and Mann, 1977)*	*Creative Production (Wallas, 1945)*	*Invention (Rossman, 1931)*
Difficulty felt	*Appraising the challenge*	*Preparation (information gathered)*	*Need or difficulty observed*
Difficulty located and defined	Specifying goals	Incubation (unconscious activity)	Problem formulated
Possible solutions suggested	Generate alternative	Illumination (solutions emerge)	Solutions formulated
Consequences considered	*Determine outcomes for each alternative*	*Verification (solutions tested and elaborated)*	*Solutions critically examined*
			New ideas formulated
Solution accepted	*Select best alternative*		*New ideas tested and selected*

that the basic unit of behavior (including thinking behavior) consists of a Test-Operate-Test-Exit sequence—a TOTE unit. This model views thinking as a feedback loop, in which a situation is evaluated (Test), the means of obtaining the desired result is produced (Operate), the situation is reevaluated (Test), and, if the results are adequate, the mind moves on to another situation (Exit).

A Definition of Critical Thinking. Critical thinking does not need to be redefined. What is needed is clarification and elaboration of a fairly loose concept. Previous definitions of critical thinking are accurate but overly restrictive, and, while the broader definitions of critical thinking provide a larger context for definition, they are so general that they provide little psychological or pedagogical guidance.

Critical thinking will be regarded here as the cognitive activity associated with the evaluation of products of thought. This cognitive activity, more accurately called critical or evaluative thought, is an essential element of problem solving, decision making, and creative production. When the mental products to be evaluated were produced by others and exist in the form of verbal statements, critical thinking often becomes the task of solving a problem or making a decision by accepting, rejecting, or modifying the statements. An assignment that calls for the identification or clarification of assumptions underlying the argument for the legalization of marijuana or that requires an examination and critique of the evidence supporting tighter regulations on the operation of nuclear reactors are examples of such tasks. The evaluative aspect of thought is also called into play when the products of one's own thinking are to be evaluated, formally or informally. The systematic weighing of topics for a term paper or even deciding where to eat lunch are examples. Furthermore, critical thinking always goes hand-in-hand with creative and productive thinking. Critical thinking can be applied to products of the visual arts, dance, and sports as well as to symbolic and verbal thought. In short, critical thinking is not a mysterious mental operation that takes place only in college classrooms but an essential component of everyday thought and deliberation.

Factors Affecting Critical Thinking

Four major factors affect one's ability to think. Three of these factors are internal; the fourth influences thinking from the outside. Knowledge and experience, relevant intellectual skills and strategies, and appropriate attitudinal dispositions work from the inside. The major external factor is the thinking environment.

Knowledge and Experience. An appropriate repertoire of knowledge and experience is a necessary condition for critical thinking. Without access to relevant facts, concepts, or principles it becomes difficult, if not impossible, to understand an argument, seek additional evidence, or evaluate information.

Two types of knowledge are important for problem solving (Greeno, 1973). The first type, propositional knowledge, refers to what people know about things. For example, a person might know that Freud describes behavior in terms of conflict between the id, the ego, and the superego or that meiosis and mitosis differ in the number and chromosome content of cells produced. The second type, algorithmic knowledge, refers to the rules or procedures for doing things. Knowing how to solve a quadratic equation or knowledge of the procedures of double-entry bookkeeping are examples of this type of knowledge.

Training that emphasizes one type of knowledge over another produces different results. For instance, Mayer and Greeno (1975) compared students' performance on mathematical problems following teaching that emphasized the use of a formula to compute answers (algorithmic knowledge) to performance following teaching that emphasized the relationship of terms in the formula to already known concepts (propositional knowledge). When students were later presented problems calling for straightforward use of simple algebraic manipulation of the formula, those who had received formula teaching did better. However, when students were asked to answer questions about the formula or to recognize unanswerable questions, those who had received general instruction did better. Since the usefulness of different types of knowledge seems to depend on what one is required to do, it seems justified to conclude that both types of knowledge are needed in order to perform effectively across a wide variety of problems.

Large or well-developed repertoires of knowledge can be advantageous to problem solvers and decision makers in a variety of ways. In some areas, expertise seems to be largely due to the accumulation of extensive bodies of propositional knowledge. For instance, Chase and Simon (1973) found that much of the difference between the ability of novice and expert chess players could be attributed to the accumulation of large bodies of chess-related knowledge by the latter. They hypothesize that chess masters have tens of thousands of visual patterns stored in their memories, so that examination of any one chess position elicits from memory similar configurations along with appropriate move selection strategies. This ability to call upon a rich internal store of information seems to be an important part of competent performance, especially in the professions. Elsewhere (Yinger, 1979, 1980), I have suggested that one important component of successful instruction is the large repertoire of teaching activities, strategies, and routines accumulated over time in instructional settings.

The development of adequate stores of propositional (or algorithmic) knowledge often takes hundreds of thousands of hours. As a result, experience, and especially practice, are major contributors to the development of skill. Johnson (1972) suggests that, in learning a principle, it is generalization of the principle on the basis of experience that facilitates its application to other problems. For example, there is no better way for students to learn the principles of computer programming than to try their hand at a few programming problems. Teachers can maximize experience by providing students with plenty of practice in the original task and by following this up with practice on similar or related tasks, a wide range of examples, and a variety of opportunities for making applications.

While there is no substitute for experience in acquiring the relevant bodies of knowledge, past experience can interfere with current thinking by causing rigidity in thinking. One example of this is the tendency, called functional-fixedness by psychologists, to attribute, as a result of experience, limited use to a potential resource. College students often have difficulty with the following problem: "Two long strings are hanging from the ceiling of an empty room. The strings are so far apart that, if you hold the end of one string, you cannot reach the other string. Devise a way to tie the ends of the two strings together using nothing more than a pair of scissors." The problem is difficult because of our tendency to think of a pair of scissors in terms of its function, cutting, and to ignore its physical attributes, such as weight. One effective way of reducing rigidity in thinking is to provide a variety of experiences with objects and materials and to provide assistance in generalizing the significance of specific experiences.

Knowledge and experience can influence thinking in a variety of ways. They can influence the way in which one perceives a situation, they can facilitate or inhibit the production of alternatives or solutions to problems, they can improve the efficiency of thinking, and they can even facilitate the learning and application of new information. One special way in which knowledge and experience come to exert such an influence on our thinking is worth mentioning. As a result of our experience, each of us has "implicit theories" about the world and the way in which it functions. Implicit theories are the unexamined or unconscious theories that allow us to structure, interpret, and make sense of our world. These informal theories are a part of our propositional knowledge and together they constitute our belief system and our personal perspective. Implicit theories become the lens and filter for everyday experience, dictating what one sees, and how one interprets it. Implicit theory becomes an executive control structure in thought (Gagné, 1974) by guiding perception, search, and storage. What is relevant or important in any given situation depends to a great extent on one's perspective on that situation. Thus, belief systems have an important role in thought and behavior (Clark and Yinger, 1977). By functioning as the organizer of knowledge and experience, implicit theory can affect one's comprehension of a situation and thereby influence critical thinking. For these reasons, efforts aimed at facilitating critical thinking in students should pay adequate attention to what the students already know.

Intellectual Skills and Strategies. Knowledge is necessary but not sufficient for successful thinking. Adequate knowledge in no way ensures proper application in problem solving (Bloom and Broder, 1950; Duncker, 1945; Maier, 1930, 1945). One must also possess skills and strategies for manipulating and processing information.

Intelligence, no doubt, is an important factor in thinking. Scores on intelligence tests correlate positively, though only moderately, with measures of general reasoning, problem solving, and critical thinking (Glaser, 1941). The relationship between measured intelligence and creativity is even less significant (Guilford and Christensen, 1973). The intellectual traits that most closely associate intelligence and thinking appear to be the ability to perform inductive reasoning and facility with abstract symbols (Burton and others, 1960). These relationships indicate that intelligence is an important factor in thinking. Nevertheless, in most cases, less than half of the individual variability in thinking can be accounted for by intelligence test scores. Evidently, there is ample room for the improvement of thinking skills in most people, regardless of their level of intelligence.

Since ancient times, intelligence and thinking skill have been equated with logic. Prior to 1900, thinking was generally regarded as a purely logical process. In this century, psychological research has revealed the importance of other processes in thought, but logic remains the central element in efforts aimed at improving thinking, especially critical thinking.

Some of the processes involved in critical thinking are more mechanical than others. Such processes as comparison, classification, and inference have been reduced to rules by logicians and philosophers, and this "logical machinery" (Beardsley, 1956) has become the cornerstone of critical thinking programs. Chapters abound devoted to logic in books that propose to foster "straight" thinking (for example, Beardsley, 1956; Black, 1952; Ennis, 1969; Organ, 1965; Thouless, 1939).

A survey of programs aimed at teaching critical thinking shows the predominance of logical skills: definition (Fawcett, 1938; Glaser, 1941; Hyram, 1957; Lewis, 1950); comprehension (Thelen, 1944); description and explanation (Peel, 1973); classification (White, 1936); interpreting data (Arnold, 1937; Glaser, 1941; Lewis, 1950; Peel, 1973; Schaaf, 1955); analyzing assumptions (Fawcett, 1938; Lewis, 1950); analyzing evidence (Fawcett, 1938; Glaser, 1941; Lewis, 1950); drawing inferences (Glaser, 1941; Hyram, 1957; Lewis, 1950; Peel, 1973;

Taba, 1966; White, 1936); judging conclusions (Fawcett, 1938; Higgins, 1945; Schaaf, 1955); and generalizing from data (Schaaf, 1955; Taba, 1966).

These authors rely heavily on the canons of logic and scientific experimentation. Much weight seems to be placed on drawing inferences (that is, on induction, deduction, and proof) and on the interpretation of data (that is, on recognizing the relevance, dependability, consistency, and adequacy of data and on detecting partiality, bias, and deception in data). There are many intellectual activities underlying these skills. I want to explore three of these activities—comprehension, information seeking, and evaluation. In order to evaluate a product of thought effectively one must be able to comprehend the meaning associated with information. Misunderstanding at this level can sabotage or nullify subsequent thought. Information seeking includes a wide variety of search and inquiry skills; it often draws upon the creative-productive aspect of thought. The third activity involves the evaluating of information. Skills related to testing, verification, and judgment of thought products belong to this activity.

Comprehension. Comprehension may be defined as the relating of new experience to what is already known (Smith, 1975). When new experience can be related to one's knowledge or previous experience, it makes sense—it is comprehended and understood. We can all remember a skilled teacher who with several carefully chosen examples or analogies could transform what we had previously regarded as nonsense into relevant and meaningful information. Comprehension forms the foundation for thinking, just as it does for learning. A prior condition for the evaluation of any product of thought is that it be understood. For this reason, comprehension is an important component of critical thinking.

The two major factors that affect comprehension are what is already known and what is seen. A problem, situation, or statement will be best understood when it is clearly perceived and then related to existing cognitive structures. The term *cognitive structure* refers to the organization and structure of the store of knowledge in our minds. Though cognitive structures have no identifiable physical properties, they are, in effect, the invisible organizational scaffolding that allows us to sort out and organize our complex world. It is the lack of a relevant cognitive structure, for instance, that makes the apparently elementary information presented in introductory courses so overwhelming to some students. Not until the basic cognitive scaffolding is set up does information begin to make sense. Not until new information can be related to information already in memory does comprehension begin to take place. For the most part, the relating of new information to existing cognitive structures takes place unconsciously. Though psychologists differ on how this relating actually occurs, it seems to involve various types of classification, matching, and assimilation processes.

Perception is dependent on knowledge, expectation, and desire; what we see is colored by what we know, by what we expect to see, and by what we would like to see (Smith, 1975). The role of perception in comprehension varies with the nature of the new information being perceived. Perception of the word *horse* is mainly dependent on knowledge, specifically on knowledge of the English language. Perception of verbal statements is is dependent not only on knowledge of syntax and vocabulary but also on expectations and desires. For instance, if you did not notice that the previous sentence contained the word *is* twice in a row, it was because you did not expect such a thing to occur in a well-edited publication. Expectation and desire play an even greater role in the peception and comprehension of more complex experiences, such as understanding a difficult problem or interpreting a work of art.

There are basically two ways of facilitating comprehension. One is to ensure that the thinker possesses an adequate and well-organized store of knowledge related to the task at hand. The other is to make the person aware of the idiosyncracies of perception. There is no way to control for the idiosyncratic influences, but there is evidence that an awareness of potential sources of bias or error can facilitate thinking ability. In a book aimed at making problem solvers aware of potential blocks to thinking, Adams (1974) lists several common sources of perceptual error. They include difficulty in isolating the problem, a tendency to delimit the problem area too closely, an inability to see the problem from various viewpoints, stereotyping (seeing only what one expects to see), visual saturation (the tendency to ignore common visual input), and the failure to use all sensory input. Knowledge of these sources of error and of strategies for overcoming them could greatly enhance perceptual and comprehension abilities.

Information Seeking. We are not simply passive reactors to our environment. Through perception, concept attainment, and reasoning, we are actively engaged in creating or constructing knowledge. One basic intellectual process that makes this possible is information seeking.

Information seeking involves us in searching for and producing information. In critical thinking, one common product of information seeking is evidence. Often, evidence is collected from existing sources. At other times, evidence must be produced. The former occurs when a student assesses the evidence that a lecturer presents to support a given point of view. The latter occurs when a student researches a particular issue for a term paper. Even when information is collected from existing sources, the arguments or statements must often be restructured to facilitate the evaluation of conclusions. Thus, all information seeking relies heavily on the productive aspect of thought.

Information seeking is directed by the questions we ask, and the questions we ask depend on how our thought is organized. Existing knowledge and its structure direct perception by directing attention, by posing "cognitive questions" (Smith, 1975).

Cognitive questions function at the level of cognitive structure and are therefore implicit or unconscious; one cannot actually put them into words. In perception, we are rarely aware of the influence of cognitive structure, but it influences thought at the conscious level as well. At some times, search processes are directed by unconscious questions or hypotheses; at other times, these questions and hypotheses are consciously formulated and become conscious guides for thought.

Not only does the structure of knowledge that we possess direct the questions that we ask, it also influences the manner in which we produce and compile the answers to these questions. Three influences merit mentioning: mode of thought, search strategy, and style.

The preferred mode of thought varies with age. Children progress from action representations, to representation through images, to a preference for symbolic representation of ideas, objects, and events (Bruner, Oliver, and Greenfield, 1966). Adults, especially in Western culture, rely almost exclusively on symbolic representation. This may be due to the heavy emphasis on verbal and mathematical thinking in Western schooling. Inflexibility in the preferred mode of thought (action, image, or symbolic mode) can affect information seeking, especially in the production of information dependent on unpracticed modes of representation. Visual thinking, for instance, is an essential thinking language for artists and designers. The number of books and courses aimed at improving visual thinking skills and strategies among students in schools of design, art, and architecture (for example, Hanks and Belliston, 1977; Hanks, Belliston, and Edwards, 1977; McKim, 1972) attests to the lack of facility in this thinking language even among individuals already skilled in these fields. The use of an incorrect problem-solving language is a major intellectual block, and fluency in several thinking languages is important for effective problem solving (Adams, 1974).

The second influence on information seeking, search strategy, represents the model or avenue chosen for information seeking. The search model changes with age, and several basic strategies have been identified by the research on problem solving. In a game of twenty questions, six-year-olds preferred to ask questions testing a self-sufficient, specific hypothesis that relies little on what has gone before (Mosher and Hornsby, 1966). This strategy is called *hypothesis scanning*. Eleven-year-olds shift to a strategy referred to as *constraint seeking*. In this approach, the thinker asks questions to eliminate as many alternatives as possible. As a strategy for information seeking, constraint seeking reflects an ability to think about several alternatives simultaneously and hierarchically that the advent of symbolic representation makes possible for older children and adults. However, neither this nor other optimal strategies are always found in adult thinkers.

One reason for the failure of many thinkers to choose optimal search strategies is inflexibility in thinking. Flexibility in thought is important in choosing a procedural strategy for producing solutions. Luchens (1942) found, for example, that once his students arrived at a formula for solving mathematical problems they relied on the formula even in cases where a simpler formula worked just as well. Hudgins (1977) suggests that this kind of rigidity can be avoided by allowing and encouraging a variety of solution procedures and by providing problems that require a variety of solving strategies. There are also resources describing possible production strategies for thinking and problem solving. Straus (1972), for instance, lists sixty-six strategies for generating ideas along with the advantages and disadvantages of each.

Flexibility also affects the production criteria used in information seeking. These are the criteria used to decide if an idea, piece of information, or alternative is relevant to the problem at hand. A very narrow view of the situation or problem can produce very narrow criteria and thus limit the generation and production of potentially useful information. The way to avoid inflexibility in this area is by encouraging a wider view of the situation, and by using some of the thinking aids suggested in "how to" books (Adams, 1974; Koberg and Bagnall, 1976) such as listing the attributes of an object or situation or consciously shifting perspectives for viewing a situation.

The third influence on information seeking is style. By style we mean the preference for certain thinking modes and for certain search strategies. Style can significantly influence the nature of information seeking. For example, constraint seeking and hypothesis scanning strategies differ in their costs and benefits for the thinker. Constraint seeking offers efficiency in the use of information and a high probability of success at the expense of cognitive work involved in planning the search strategy and building the required conceptual structure. In comparison, hypothesis scanning costs less in cognitive work and increases the chance of an immediate payoff, but it also increases the risk of overlooking a possibility for want of a conceptual structure. The probability of obtaining useful information must be weighed against the work required to obtain it. The amount of information collected before a solution is found also differs from thinker to thinker. For most people, this seems to be a matter of information-seeking style. Activities ranging from solving verbal analogies (Westcott, 1968) to the decision making of teachers (Shulman and others, 1968) show style differences.

Certain aspects of information seeking style are a matter of personal preference. Nevertheless, the fact that style reflects the tendency of an individual to rely on some modes of thought or search strategies in preference to others makes it of concern to teachers who are interested in facilitating critical thinking. The dangers involved in the use of inappropriae or incorrect solving languages and in the inflexible use of a given search strategy should be relayed to students so that they question the appropriateness of the modes of thought and search strategies that they routinely apply to the particular problem being addressed.

Evaluation. Information that is produced without being evaluated is an unfinished performance, like a cake that is baked but not tasted. The evaluation of thought products is a judgment activity involving the processes of comparison and decision. New information is compared with existing information according to specified criteria, and the result of this comparison is used to make a decision concerning criterion satisfaction. Judgment comes into play at several points in most intellectual activities. Judgment is involved in recognition of the situation or problem (What am I to do here? Have I seen this problem before?), in determining the applicability or relevance of an information source in weighing evidence (Is this data relevant? Does this information support the argument?), and in determining progress toward a solution (How close am I to having this problem licked? Have my efforts resulted in a step toward the solution?).

There is a variety of criteria that may be used as the basis for evaluation or judgment. Psychologists have determined three types of criteria: logical, perceptual, and affective (Guilford, 1967; Johnson, 1972).

The logical criteria include those most often referred to in writings on critical thinking. These criteria are heavily relied on in the weighing and evaluation of evidence. Guilford's (1967) study of the structure and operations of the intellect identified numerous logical criteria applied to the evaluation of products of thought. The three most common criteria are identity (Is this meaning of this argument identical with the meaning of that one?), similarity (Is this finding similar to other findings in this context?), and consistency (Is this statement consistent with other related statements?). Additional criteria identified by Guilford include satisfaction of class membership, completeness, fulfillment of implications, internal consistency, and interpretability.

Perceptual criteria may be called upon in judging figural or visual products. Symmetry, balance, simplicity, originality, esthetic value, and good form are only a few of the criteria used in perceptual judgment. These are common bases for evaluation and criticism in architecture, design engineering, and the fine arts.

Affective criteria are involved in moral and ethical evaluations and in determining the subjective, personal value or utility of alternatives. These criteria include such things as pleasure, satisfaction, and comfort. They are applied not only in ethics courses but whenever we have to make a judgment or decision that affects us personally, such as when buying a car, choosing a vocation, or deciding what movie to see.

Most judgments involve criteria from more than one category. For this reason, teachers need to alert students to the variety of criteria that may be brought to bear on any one problem. There seems to be a tendency in higher education to emphasize logical criteria at the expense of the others. Nevertheless, perceptual and affective criteria play an important role in all fields—even in the so-called hard sciences. Robert March (1978, pp. 1-2), in his book *Physics for Poets* illustrates this point.

> Like many poets, the physicist feels he is looking for "truth." Of course, he defines truth by his own set of rules, and he doesn't think very much about what those rules are (until he gets old, when good physicists often turn into bad philosophers). Thus, he may be just as surprised to hear that some of those rules have to do with beauty. An idea must be more than right—it must be pretty if it is to create much excitement in the world of physics. Creativity in any field has an emotional dimension. This may seem surprising, in view of what we are always told about the rules of scientific objectivity. But these rules only concern the way in which an idea gets its final test. The way in which a new idea arises is usually quite the opposite of objective. And if the idea strikes the audience as beautiful, it is likely to be believed even in the absence of confirming evidence and clung to tenaciously until the evidence against it is overwhelming. The creator of an abstract scientific idea has as much of his personality in it as any artist.

Three factors play a major role in judgment or evaluation abilities. The first factor is one's store of knowledge. Since evaluation involves the comparison of new information with what is already known, one's store of knowledge and the way in which it is organized can strongly influence judgment processes. The previous discussion of how the knowledge that we already have influences our thinking underlined the enormous influence that is exerted on thought by the knowledge and experience we bring to any problem or decision.

Practice is the second factor that influences evaluation. Judgment of creative products, for example, improves as a result of practice in producing similar products. In one study (Johnson and Zerbolio, 1964), criteria for cleverness were clarified by efforts to produce clever titles for story plots. Exposure to ideas of different levels of quality, explanations of differences in quality, and practice in judging ideas, accompanied by feedback, improved the ability to judge solutions to problems (Johnson and others, 1968). Studies of judgment making indicate that practice sensitizes us to the relevance of various criteria to evaluation and allows us to be more effective in applying them.

The third factor in judgment ability is knowledge of the logical mistakes that are typically made in reasoning. College courses in logic and other efforts at improving reasoning abilities deal directly with the common fallacies of thinking. Such fallacies include the use of insufficient or nonrepresentative instances, ignorance of contradictory information, false assumptions, and irrelevant appeals or arguments.

One of the most complex, yet common, judgments that we are called on to make is the assessment of probabilities and the prediction of the values of uncertain quantities. Whenever we make decisions based on beliefs concerning the likelihood of uncertain events (Shall I take my raincoat to work with me today? Is this a safe investment? Will this problem go away if I ignore it?) we are making these kinds of judgments. In psychological research on these judgments (Tversky and Kahneman, 1974), three commonly used heuristic principles that many people rely upon have been identified. They are representativeness, availability, and adjustment and anchoring.

The representativeness heuristic is commonly called into effect by questions like: What is the probability that object A belongs to Class B? or, What is the probability that event A originates from or leads to event B? To answer these questions people typically evaluate these probabilities by the degree to which A resembles B. Judging a person's intelligence by the degree to which his or her appearance matches one's stereotype of an intelligent person would be an example of the use of this heuristic. Judging probability on the basis of similarity can lead to serious errors in judgment, because this heuristic is insensitive to factors that should affect probability judgments, such as how often an event has occurred in the past, the size of the sample yielding the information, and the reliability of information.

When asked to assess the probability that an event will occur, people commonly rely on the heuristic of availability. This heuristic relies upon the "ease with which instances or occurrences can be brought to mind. For example, one may assess the risk of heart attack among middle-aged people by recalling such occurrences among one's acquaintances" (Tversky and Kahneman, 1974, p. 1127). This heuristic, however, can be biased by how easy it is to retrieve certain information from memory, by how effective one's memory search strategies are, and by the frequency of co-occurrence of two events.

When asked to estimate frequencies of occurrence (for example, What percent of African countries belong to the United Nations?) by making adjustments from an initial value of starting point, people tend to be over-cautious in their revisions and biased toward the initial view.

This is the heuristic of adjustment and anchoring, and is generally due to our tendency to be too conservative in our willingness to review our predictions based on the information available. Knowledge of each of these errors has been shown to reduce the tendency to make them; thus training in an awareness of errors should be an important part of any effort to improve critical thinking.

Attitudes and Dispositions. Psychologists have proposed many definitions of attitude, but most would agree that an attitude is some type of learned or acquired state that influences personal choice and action. One realm of choice and action in which attitudes seem especially influential is thinking. Burton and others (1960) list ten attitudes critical for good thinking: intellectual curiosity, intellectual honesty, objectivity, intelligent skepticism, open-mindedness, conviction of universal cause-and-effect relationships, disposition to be systematic, flexibility, persistence, and decisiveness. Hudgins (1977, p. 178) suggests that one key attitude for effective critical thinking is a "disposition to search for evidence which bears upon an argument or the conclusions drawn from an argument. Such an attitude should pervade the behavior of the learner whenever he is asked to accept a conclusion . . . wanting to know what evidence is available . . . is a hallmark of critical thinking."

In what may be the most famous study of problem solving among college students, Bloom and Broder (1950) found that good and poor problem solvers showed distinct differences in their attitudes toward problems and solutions. Good problem solvers were more aggressive, confident, tenacious, and attentive to detail. They placed their faith in reason, rather than in guessing. In contrast, the efforts of poor problem solvers were characterized by lack of attention to detail, unreasoned guessing, and self-justification.

Personal values and biases exert a strong influence on thinking and may even become "emotional blocks" (Adams, 1974) to effective thinking. Values and biases reflect our cognitive structure and implicit theories. They color all aspects of our thinking, but their influence is especially strong in situations that call for judgments or decisions about affective or emotionally toned subject matter. For example, college students were asked to judge whether the conclusions reached by a series of syllogisms were warranted by the statements given in support of them (Lefford, 1946, pp. 130–131). Syllogisms that involved controversial issues, such as "War times are prosperous times, and prosperity is highly desirable, therefore, wars are much to be desired," were judged correctly less often than syllogisms that matched them in form but contained noncontroversial content, such as "All whales live in water, and all fish live in water, therefore, all fish must be whales."

Other attitudes that become emotional blocks to effective thinking are fear of making a mistake or failing, inability to tolerate ambiguity or disorder, a disposition toward premature judgment, and a need for quick success (Adams, 1974).

Finally, all critical thinkers benefit from the general attitude described by Koberg and Bagnall (1976, p. 12), called "constructive discontent":

> Arrival at the age of sixteen is usually all that is required for achieving half of this important attribute of creativity. It is unusual to find a "contented" young person; discontent goes with that time of life. To the young, everything needs improvement. . . . As we age, our discontent wanes; we learn from society that "fault-finders" disturb the status quo of the normal, average "others." Squelch tactics are introduced. It becomes "good" not to "make waves" or "rock the boat" and to "let sleeping dogs lie" and "be seen but not heard." It is "good" to be invisible and enjoy your "autonomy." It is "bad" to be a problem maker. And so everything is upside down for creativity and its development. Thus, constructive attitudes are necessary for a dynamic condition; discontent is a prerequisite to problem solving. Combined, they define a primary quality of the creative problem solver: a constantly developing constructive discontent.

As Adams (1974, p. 77) says, "This questioning attitude can be achieved by conscious effort. One merely needs to start questioning." Teachers can facilitate positive attitudes toward thinking and reasoning by alerting students to these influences and by modeling these attitudes in their own approach to issues and problems in their subject matter and courses.

The Thinking Environment. All thinking takes place in a context—an environment exerting physical, social, and intellectual forces that surround and offset the individual. Although we may try to resist the influences of our surroundings, it is rare for us to escape these pervasive forces completely. This is especially true of school situations. Students' thoughts and behavior seem extremely susceptible to influences inside and outside classrooms.

The physical environment affects thinking primarily by facilitating or inhibiting concentration. We have all experienced difficulty in thinking that has resulted from a cold room, the noise from a television set, whispers from people in another part of the classroom, or blue sky seen through the window. The effects of environmental stimuli are subject to wide individual differences; one person's distractor may be another person's facilitator. This is especially true for the effects of the physical environment on productive thought. Some people are most creative or productive when surrounded by such generally conducive environmental influences as soft music or low lights. Others require more extreme influences. Kant did some of his best thinking in bed with the blankets wrapped around him in a special way; Dr. Johnson needed a purring cat, orange peel, and tea; and Schiller filled his desk with rotten apples. Teachers do not need to resort to these extremes to foster critical thinking; a physical environment free of distractions will suffice.

However, in most thinking situations, the major environmental influences are not physical but emotional and intellectual. Support that can be offered in these areas is important to all aspects of thought. Two mechanisms for providing such support in school situations are the instructions given to students and teacher attitudes.

Students spend a lot of time and effort determining what the teacher wants them to do. Questions like "Will this be on the exam?" reflect the students' sensitivity to the directions for learning provided by instructors. In general, instructions given prior to productive thought have significant effects on both the quality and quantity of ideas produced (Johnson, 1972). Even brief and rather ambiguous instructions like "be creative" or "stop and think" seem to influence thought processes and products (Manske and Davis, 1968).

The teacher's attitude is the other important avenue for conveying support to students as they learn to think critically. Creative performace was highest among school children in classrooms of teachers who had favorable attitudes toward creativity (Torrance, 1965), while anecdotal evidence provides support for the notion that critical thinking is facilitated in situations where teachers are strongly dedicated to encouraging critical thinking in students (Fawcett, 1938; Grener and Raths, 1945). Although the evidence for specific environmental influences on critical thinking is limited, we can infer from the work on productive thinking that one important way in which critical thinking programs influence students' thought is by creating an environment that encourages and supports these mental processes.

Putting It All Together: The Skills of the Practical

Johnson (1972, p. 227) observed that "the teaching of problem solving is much like prescientific farming. Some teachers are more successful than others; and much good advice can be had for the asking." Many observers would say that the teaching of critical thinking is at the same state. Such comments suggest, as farming already has, that the psychology and pedagogy of thinking can and soon will move into the scientific age. By careful observation and assessment of factors affecting thinking and by continued fine tuning of training methods, hardy error-resistant strains of thinking can be produced.

This technological-engineering point of view is already reflected in many programs aimed at improving critical thinking. These programs emphasize intellectual skills, especially the logical machinery of thought mentioned earlier. However, this approach holds a danger for students, if students develop the erroneous impression that most problems can be solved through procedural means.

Most of the problems that we encounter in daily life are practical rather than theoretical and uncertain rather than procedural. "Who should I vote for?" "Which wallpaper would look best in the kitchen?" Such problems as these are instances of what Gauther (1963) has labeled "uncertain practical problems." Reid (1979, pp. 188–189) attributes the following characteristics to practical problems: they have to be answered, even if the answer is to decide to do nothing; the grounds on which the solution is to be based are uncertain; some existing state of affairs must always be taken into account; they are always unique, and their particulars can never be exhaustively described; they require us to adjudicate between competing goals and values; and, whatever the solution we reach, its outcome cannot be predicted, not can we know the outcome that would have resulted from a different solution.

Although some practical problems are amenable to procedural treatment, the general hallmark of practical problems is uncertainty. A problem can be classified as procedural if a solution can be obtained by calculation or by the application of an appropriate algorithm. For instance, if we have already decided where to spend our holiday, the practical problem of how to get to the place we have chosen may turn out to be routinely soluble; we check route maps or railway timetables to find the answer that fits our requirements.

There is a tendency in today's society to avoid the difficulties raised by uncertain problems ("What should I do?") by reducing uncertain problems to procedural problems. This tendency is due in part to an overreliance on procedural methods and techniques to compensate for lack of experience in dealing with uncertain practical problems. Aylesworth and Reagan (1969, p. 4) define critical thinking as "the mental skill of solving problems in the manner of the practitioner." That is, critical thinking encourages the student to act as a practitioner rather than an observer. To function as a practitioner, the student must be able to deal with uncertain practical problems.

The skills that practitioners need are the skills of practical deliberation. This involves the accumulation of knowledge, skills, and attitudes conducive to handling practical problems and decisons. Reid (1979) identifies two components necessary for developing practical problem-solving skills: the refinement of a stock of knowledge as the result of artful practice and contemplation, and the extension, elaboration, and refinement of criteria for judgment and action. I would add to these a third component: appropriate attitudes for dealing with complexity and uncertainty in everyday problems.

To develop these skills of practical deliberation, teachers need to become more aware of how knowledge and skills develop and of what they can do to encourage critical and creative thinking. In this chapter, I have argued that we should broaden our approaches for improving students' thinking by acknowledging the nature of the problems that they will most frequently encounter and by supplementing the existing emphasis on procedural techniques with knowledge, skills, and attitudes that will be needed to solve uncertain practical problems. To achieve this aim, efforts to improve the critical and evaluative aspects of thought must be better integrated with efforts aimed at improving the productive and creative aspects of thought. At the same time, we should provide practice in using and integrating these skills in practical situations as well as in theoretical situations.

Every day, we see changes brought about by the increased application of the computer as a thinking machine. Computers are very good at solving procedural problems, and it is to these problems that computers are most often applied. However, computers are very poor at solving practical problems, because these problems require abilities far beyond the procedural. As the role of computers expands, the thinking that will be in greatest demand from tomorrow's generation will be creative and critical thinking in practical problems. If we choose, we can prepare students for that role today.

References

Adams, J. L. *Conceptual Blockbusting: A Guide to Better Ideas.* San Francisco: Freeman, 1974.

Arnold, O. L. "Testing Ability to Use Data in the Fifth and Sixth Grades." *Educational Research Bulletin,* 1937, *17,* 225–259, 278.

Aylesworth, T. G., and Reagan, G. M. *Teaching for Thinking.* New York: Doubleday, 1969.

Beardsley, M. C. *Thinking Straight.* Englewood Cliffs, N.J.: Prentice-Hall, 1956.

Black, M. *Critical Thinking.* (2nd ed.) Englewood Cliffs, N.J.: Prentice-Hall, 1956.

Bloom, B. S. *Stability and Change in Human Characteristics.* New York: Wiley, 1964.

Bloom, B. S., and Broder, L. J. *Problem-Solving Processes of College Students: An Exploratory Investigation.* Supplementary Educational Monographs, No. 73. Chicago: University of Chicago Press, 1950.

Bruner, J., Oliver, R., and Greenfield, P. *Studies in Cognitive Growth.* New York: Wiley, 1966.

Burton, W. H., and others. *Education for Effective Thinking.* New York: Appleton-Century-Crofts, 1960.

Chase, W. G., and Simon, H. A. "The Mind's Eye in Chess." In W. G. Chase (Ed.), *Visual Information Processing.* New York: Wiley, 1973.

Clark, C. M., and Yinger, R. J. "Research on Teacher Thinking." *Curriculum Inquiry,* 1977, *7* (4), 279–304.

Dewey, J. *How We Think.* Lexington, Mass.: Heath, 1933.

Duncker, K. "On Problem Solving." *Psychological Monographs,* 1945, *58,* 270.

Ennis, R. H. "A Concept of Critical Thinking." *Harvard Educational Review,* 1962, *32,* 81–111.

Ennis, R. H. *Logic in Teaching.* Englewood Cliffs, N.J.: Prentice-Hall, 1969.

Fawcett, H. P. *The Nature of Proof.* 13th Yearbook, National Council of Teachers of Mathematics. New York: Teachers College, Columbia University, 1938.

Gagné, R. M. *Essentials of Learning for Instruction.* Hinsdale, Ill.: Dryden Press, 1974.

Gauther, D. P. *Practical Reasoning: The Structure and Foundations of Prudential and Moral Arguments and Their Exemplification in Discourse.* London: Oxford University Press, 1963.

Glaser, E. M. "An Experiment in the Development of Critical Thinking." *Teachers College Contributions to Education,* No. 843. New York: Bureau of Publications, Teachers College, Columbia University, 1941.

Greeno, J. G. "The Structure of Memory and the Process of Solving Problems." In R. L. Solso (Ed.), *Contemporary Issues in Cognitive Psychology.* Washington, D.C.: Winston, 1973.

Grener, N., and Raths, L. "Thinking in Grade 3." *Educational Research Bulletin,* 1945, *24,* 38–42.

Guilford, J. P. *The Nature of Human Intelligence.* New York: McGraw-Hill, 1967.

Guilford, J. P., and Christensen, P. R. "The One-Way Relation Between Creative Potential and I.Q." *Journal of Creative Behavior,* 1973, *7,* 247–252.

Guilford, J. P., Kettner, N. W., and Christensen, P. R. "The Nature of the General Reasoning Factor." *Psychological Review,* 1956, *63,* 169–172.

Hanks, K., and Belliston, L. *Draw! A Visual Approach to Thinking, Learning, and Communicating.* Los Altos, Calif.: Kaufmann, 1977.

Hanks, K., Belliston, L., and Edwards, D. *Design Yourself.* Los Altos, Calif.: Kaufmann, 1977.

Higgins, C. D. "The Educability of Adolescents in Inductive Ability." *Science Education,* 1945, *22,* 82–85.

Hudgins, B. B. *Learning and Thinking.* Itaska, Ill.: Peacock, 1977.

Hyram, G. H. "An Experiment in Developing Critical Thinking in Children." *Journal of Experimental Education,* 1957, *26,* 125–132.

Janis, I. L., and Mann, L. *Decision Making: A Psychological Analysis of Conflict, Choice, and Commitment.* New York: Free Press, 1977.

Johnson, D. M. *A Systematic Introduction to the Psychology of Thinking.* New York: Harper & Row, 1972.

Johnson, D. M., and others. "Production and Judgment of Solutions to Five Problems." *Journal of Educational Psychology,* 1968, *59,* Monograph Supplement No. 6.

Johnson, D. M., and Zerbolio, D. J. "Relations Between Production and Judgments of Plot Titles." *American Journal of Psychology,* 1964, *77,* 99–105.

Kneller, G. F. *The Art and Science of Creativity.* New York: Holt, Rinehart and Winston, 1965.

Koberg, D., and Bagnall, J. *The Universal Traveler: A Soft-System Guide to Creativity, Problem-Solving, and the Process of Reaching Goals.* Los Altos, Calif.: Kaufmann, 1976.

Lefford, A. "The Influence of Emotional Subject Matter on Logical Reasoning." *Journal of General Psychology,* 1946, *34,* 127–151.

Lewis, H. "An Experiment in Developing Critical Thinking Through the Teaching of Plane Demonstrative Geometry." *Mathematics Teacher,* 1950, *43,* 411–413.

Luchens, A. S. "Mechanization in Problem Solving." *Psychological Monographs,* 1942, *54,* 248.

McKim, R. H. *Experiences in Visual Thinking.* Monterey, Calif.: Brooks/Cole, 1972.

Maier, N. R. F. "Reasoning in Humans. I. On Direction." *Journal of Comparative Psychology,* 1930, *11,* 114–143.

Maier, N. R. F. "Reasoning in Humans. III. The Mechanisms of Equivalent Stimuli and of Reasoning." *Journal of Experimental Psychology,* 1945, *35,* 349–360.

Manske, E., and Davis, G. A. "Effects of Simple Instructional Biases upon Performance in the Unusual Uses Test." *Journal of General Psychology,* 1968, *79,* 25–33.

March, R. H. *Physics for Poets.* (2nd ed.) New York: McGraw-Hill, 1978.

Mayer, R. E., and Greeno, J. G. "Structural Differences Between Learning Outcomes Produced by Different Instructional Methods." *Journal of Educational Psychology,* 1975, *67,* 331–350.

Merrifield, P. R., and others. "The Role of Intellectual Factors in Problem Solving." *Psychological Monographs,* 1962, *76,* 529.
Miller, G. A., Galanter, E., and Pribram, K. H. *Plans and the Structure of Behavior.* New York: Holt, Rinehart and Winston, 1960.
Mosher, F. A., and Hornsby, J. R. "On Asking Questions." In J. S. Bruner, R. R. Oliver, and P. M. Greenfield (Eds.), *Studies in Cognitive Growth.* New York: Wiley, 1966.
Organ, T. W. *The Art of Critical Thinking.* Boston: Houghton Mifflin, 1965.
Peel, E. A. *The Nature of Adolescent Judgment.* New York: Wiley-Interscience, 1973.
Reid, W. A. "Practical Reasoning and Curriculum Theory: In Search of a New Paradigm." *Curriculum Inquiry,* 1979, *9,* 187-207.
Rossman, J. *The Psychology of the Inventor.* Washington, D.C.: Inventors Publishing, 1931.
Schaaf, O. "Student Discovery of Algebraic Principles as a Means of Developing Ability to Generalize." *Mathematics Teacher,* 1955, *48,* 324-327.
Shulman, L. S., and others. *Studies of the Inquiry Process: Inquiry Patterns of Students in Teacher Training Programs.* Final report, Office of Education Project No. 5-0597. East Lansing: Michigan State University, 1968.
Simon, H. A. *Administrative Behavior: A Study of Decision-Making Processes in Administrative Organizations.* (3rd ed.) New York: Free Press, 1976.
Smith, F. *Comprehension and Learning: A Conceptual Framework for Teachers.* New York: Holt, Rinehart and Winston, 1975.
Straus, D. *Strategy Notebook.* San Francisco: Interaction Associates, 1972.
Taba, H. *Teaching Strategies and Cognitive Functioning in Elementary School Children.* Cooperative Research Project No. 2404. San Francisco: San Francisco State University, 1966.
Thelen, H. A. "A Methodological Study of the Learning of Chemical Concepts and of Certain Abilities to Think Critically in Freshman Chemistry." *Journal of Experimental Education,* 1944, *13,* 53-75.
Thouless, R. H. *How to Think Straight.* New York: Hart, 1939.
Torrance, E. P. *Rewarding Creative Behavior.* Englewood Cliffs, N.J.: Prentice-Hall, 1965.
Tversky, A., and Kahneman, D. "Judgment Under Uncertainty: Heuristics and Biases." *Science,* 1974, *185,* 1124-1131.
Wallas, G. *The Art of Thought.* London: Watts, 1945.
Westcott, M. R. *Psychology of Intuition.* New York: Holt, Rinehart and Winston, 1968.
White, E. E. "A Study of the Possibility of Improving Habits of Thought in School Children by a Training of Logic." *British Journal of Educational Psychology,* 1936, *6,* 267-273.
Yinger, R. J. "Routines in Teacher Planning." *Theory Into Practice,* 1979, *18,* 163-169.
Yinger, R. J. "A Study of Teacher Planning." *The Elementary School Journal,* 1980, *80,* 107-127.

Robert J. Yinger is an assistant professor of education at the University of Cincinnati, who for the past three years has been pursuing a program of research on teacher planning initiated when he was a research associate at the Institute for Research on Teaching at Michigan State University. Also among his interests are cognitive psychology and instructional theory.

Four approaches to teaching problem solving—an important aspect of critical thinking—have gained recent notice with their success.

Strategies for Problem Solving

Jerry K. Stonewater

John Holt once said that children are by nature smart, curious, eager to learn, and good at it; they learn best when they are happy, active, involved, and interested in what they are doing. Periodically, I see students like that. However, I teach mathematics and problem solving and I often get discouraged, because my students are not always smart, curious, or eager to learn.

Yet in my more upbeat moments I remember those glorious times in the classroom when a student made that breakthrough—"Aha! I see it now . . . ." These times bring me back to serious thinking about the teaching and learning of problem solving. Although I am never really sure whether the "aha" resulted from divine intervention, sheer luck, or my very careful and selective instruction, I do think that research is making it clear what we can do to increase the probability that the "aha" results from instruction and not from luck or divine intervention. Hence, my intent in this chapter is to describe four approaches for teaching problem solving that have worked for student learning.

First I describe the Guided Design strategy developed by Charles E. Wales and Robert A. Stager at West Virginia University, an approach to problems that require creative and/or divergent solutions. The focus of Guided Design is on the process of problem solving, in that it encourages students to identify problems, list constraints and assumptions, and generate alternative solutions.

The second approach, the University of Nebraska ADAPT program, is a multidisciplinary freshman-year program based on Piaget's theory of cognitive growth. The program's primary focus is on the development of students' thinking or reasoning capabilities, especially those necessary for solving complex academic and practical problems.

Moshe Rubinstein's work at UCLA provides the third approach, which stresses the content that reduces uncertainty in decision making for problem solving. Lastly, John Roueche's summary of remedial programs is considered. Although remedial programs may seem out of place here, they have importance for problem solving because they can provide students with the prerequisites necessary to begin solving complex problems, especially by developing attitudes that facilitate readiness for learning.

I will describe how each of these four strategies pursues its special focus. Each strategy is described from three viewpoints: how it works, the roles that students and professors play, and the evidence for its effectiveness.

These strategies suggest the major components of successful problem-solving instruction. As self-contained approaches in particular disciplines and particular colleges, they have achieved surprising results. I will follow my descriptions with a synthesis of those features of the teaching of problem solving which may be applicable whenever we wish to assist students in this important aspect of critical thinking.

Guided Design

Consider the following problem, which was recently used in a junior-level guided design engineering department course on thermodynamics: "Four friends set out on an overnight fishing trip in the Gulf and everything went well the first day. However, during the night, a strong wind pulled the anchor free and the boat drifted to a nearby island. Its propeller was broken, but there were oars in the boat. The group also had a windbreaker, one poncho, a sleeping bag, sunglasses, a cooler with two bottles of pop per person, matches, a compass, and a salt shaker. Given this list, rank order the items in their importance to the survival of the group."

If you are thinking that this problem hardly sounds like thermodynamics, you are correct. This type of problem is used as an introduction to the guided design approach, which emphasizes the *process* of problem solving. Later, after students are comfortable with the process, course-relevant problems emerge. The method is simple. It engages a specific problem-solving procedure (that is, the process) and the subject material of the course. The faculty members who have designed and used the strategy claim to teach both problem-solving processes and content information—two goals of instruction that stubbornly resist integration—effectively.

Strategy Description. The problem-solving procedure is the focal point of a guided design course. It includes eleven steps: identifying the problem; stating the problem objective; listing constraints, assumptions, and facts; generating possible solutions; determining the most likely solution; analyzing, synthesizing, and evaluating the solution; and reporting, implementing, and checking results. The steps are sequenced for optimal problem solving, and each can be seen in and of itself as a miniproblem that allows students to experience real-world problem complexities.

A second set of directions for the survival problem quoted above illustrates this idea of miniproblem. Students are asked to list solutions to the survival problem. Suggestions include: row to shore, stay on the island, gather wood, build a fire, ration food and water, and catch fish. Students soon discover that each could be a solution to a different problem, and that the first step in the problem-solving procedure must be to identify the problem. They learn to short-circuit a real-world dilemma that often is a difficulty for problem solvers—clear definition or identification of the problem.

The second component of a guided design course, the content, does not hold the traditional place of honor that it has in most courses. Neither the planning of a guided design course nor its delivery depends solely on the content; both planning and delivery depend, rather, on a series of problems, which are selected and designed to reflect application of the necessary content. Once the content objectives have been selected, problems that are based upon the content can be identified. The course becomes the solving of these problems by use of the eleven steps in the problem-solving procedure. By constructing the course as a series of problems to be solved rather than as a series of lectures to be listened to and memorized, instructors can use problem solving as the vehicle for the learning of content, rather than the contrary.

The survival problem shows how the problem-solving process of guided design teaches content. One content objective at this point in a guided design course is for students to recognize the importance of correctly identifying and stating the problem before they attempt a solution. There is probably not one single student alive who has not been told that problem identification is a critical step in problem solving, yet students still fail to apply the step in problem solving. The guided design process teaches this idea via problem solving.

Students also learn course content as they work in groups at their own speed to solve given problems. Lectures are seldom given, so the material must be learned outside of class time, by self-instruction (readings, slides, tapes, audio-tutorial materials, and so forth). Class time is devoted to group problem solving and testing. Problems are carefully designed to require knowledge of the content in order to motivate students to learn it. In order to solve a problem utilizing the first law of thermodynamics, students must first learn the law.

Most of the problems presented in a guided design course have more than one plausible solution. This makes the professor's critique and assistance necessary if students are to improve their problem-solving behavior. After completing each step in the process, the student group receives feedback sheets, which contain one or two possible solutions and an analysis of the strengths and weaknesses of each solution. Groups compare and contrast their solutions with the professor's. Not until the professor agrees that the group's solution is adequate can the group proceed to the next step. A mastery, self-paced system emerges, based upon constant feedback and modeling from the instructor.

Another example (Wales and Stager, 1977) may help clarify the process. Students are shown a road sign, "Bridge Freezes Before Road Surface," and told to solve the problem. Not knowing the actual problem, they begin by applying the first step in the process—identifying the problem. The instructions for this step pose the question, "Does the sign identify a problem or is it a solution to another problem?"

After the students discuss the question and posit their own answers, the professor responds and students evaluate the appropriateness of their answers. In this case, that the bridge freezes before the road freezes is not the problem; rather, the freezing causes ice to form, which creates a hazard for cars, and this is the actual problem. This type problem points students to the subtleties of problem identification.

Next, students list the constraints of the problem—safety, economics, and feasibility. Possible solutions are generated and ranked according to these three constraints. Feedback sheets at this point help students see that some solutions satisfy one constraint but not others. A proposal to move the bridge to Florida—this was actually suggested in one case—may satisfy the safety criterion, but it is certainly not economical or feasible. Another proposed solution, putting insulation under the bridge, satisfies all three criteria. Hence, it would be ranked above moving the bridge to Florida.

The analysis step requires separation of the chosen solution into meaningful parts, each of which needs to be considered. One part of the solution would be to experiment with various types of insulation to determine which was best under various conditions. Another part would be to gather estimates of the cost of labor for insulating the bridge. All these various components are considered during the analysis phase.

The synthesis step recombines the parts, the information gathered, and any data that have been generated in order to create a detailed solution. The information that has been gathered on the variables of type and thickness would be used to determine the specifications for insulation to use in solving this problem.

Finally, the results are evaluated against the previously stated criteria of safety, economics, and feasibility.

The major components of guided design are the process; the content, which is learned outside of class via self-instructional materials; and the problems that are to be solved with the aid of the process once the prerequisite content has been mastered. Students work in self-paced groups and demonstrate successful completion of each process step, while the instructor provides detailed modeling and feedback at every step.

Role of the Professor. The role of the professor in a guided design course is vastly different from the professor's role in a traditional lecture and discussion course. That role can best be described as one of process planner, consultant, facilitator, and quality control supervisor.

As a process planner, the professor organizes and designs the course. Instead of the usual methods used in preparing a lecture, the professor constructs problems based on the selected content, devises self-instructional materials for content learning, and prepares feedback sheets for each process step in each problem. These planning activities require a great deal of creative thought, and time is required to coordinate and sequence the problems and the content assignments so that prerequisites are completed, problems are meaningful, and feedback is appropriate.

The professor's consultant and facilitator functions take place in the classroom and include such tasks as providing information to groups, encouraging groups when they fall behind, and asking leading questions to stimulate thinking. Seldom does the professor disseminate information in a lecture, but information can be given if the class is off-track or if one group finds a particularly good solution that should be shared with the rest of the class.

The quality control aspect of the professor's role is especially meaningful in relationship to the feedback that is given to students. Both the printed feedback and the oral communication with each group must provide helpful information, but they must also serve to redirect groups that have derived solutions of poor quality. Failure to provide adequate quality control leads to inadequate solutions.

Role of the Student. As in any instructional approach that requires active involvement, the student's role in a guided design course is vulnerable. The guided design student cannot hide in a lecture. The student must be willing to contribute to and help to develop effective group communication skills, particularly the skills of listening, paraphrasing, and compromising. The student is required to function both as tutor, when explaining a particular insight to others, and as tutee, when he or she does not understand. Guided design requires that time out of class be spent studying content material. Above all, competence in problem solving must be developed; the most noteworthy element of this competence is the ability to apply the steps of the process. In short, the student is required to be an active learner, to communicate ideas within a group, to work outside of class to learn content, to learn problem-solving skills, and to be receptive to a new type of learning experience.

Results. The results of guided design instruction are impressive. Four major trends emerge for students who have completed a guided design course when they are compared to students who have not: the attrition rate is lower; students' grades at graduation are higher; they see themselves as more in control of their environment; and they evidence less anxiety.

Wales and Stager indicate that the attrition rates had reached 60 percent before guided design was introduced as a freshman requirement in the engineering curriculum at West Virginia University. After its introduction, attrition fell to 44 percent. These authors report that the attrition rate at other engineering schools during the same period hovered around 60 percent and that ACT and high school grade point averages of students in the study remained fairly constant.

Grade point averages at graduation were higher for engineering students who took guided design than for those who did not. Also, the grade point averages of engineering graduates who took guided design were higher than those of all University graduates. This was true also of freshman grades. These results are especially meaningful in view of the fact that engineering students traditionally have lower grade point averages than all other groups of students.

In the personal and psychological realm, Tseng and Wales (1972) report that, after taking the guided design course, students felt more in control of events and evidenced a decrease in anxiety. The authors attribute these results to the design of the course—students study content on their own, correct their own homework and quizzes, and have an opportunity to retest hourly exams until mastery is achieved.

Summary. Guided design is an instructional approach that utilizes one particular problem-solving process as the primary tool for integrating the learning of content and problem-solving skills. Professors are planners, facilitators, and quality-control experts. Students are active learners: they solve problems in groups, learn content by self-instruction, and grow into effective problem solvers. Attrition and anxiety are decreased, while grades rise and feelings of control are increased.

ADAPT

Forty-two to 89 percent of college students cannot reason at levels required by the university curriculum. This fact may be the most consistent finding of recent research on college learners (Elkind, 1962; Griffiths, 1973; McKinnon, 1970; Stonewater, 1977; Tower and Wheatley, 1971). It also squares with the experience of any number of professors who work closely with students. As a result, faculty members at the University of Nebraska decided to take an approach which has as its premise that many, if not most, students are deficient in abstract reasoning skills. They created a strategy, called the ADAPT program, to help students develop abstract reasoning skills.

Strategy Description. The ADAPT faculty has focused on the activities and experiences that help students to develop the thinking skills necessary for successful completion of college. The multidisciplinary freshman program emphasizes reasoning skill development as well as content learning, but, as with guided design, content learning is secondary. In the program, "content is determined as much by its usefulness in promoting reasoning as by its importance in the content scheme of the discipline" (Fuller, 1977, p. 6).

Students who enroll in ADAPT spend their entire freshman year in the program, which includes thirty semester hours in anthropology, economics, English, history, mathematics, and physics. Again, the basic assumption followed in design of each course is that most college instruction assumes a level of reasoning that many college students have yet to develop.

The ADAPT strategy takes much of its form from the ideas of the Swiss psychologist Jean Piaget. Piaget (1952) claims that cognitive development proceeds through four unvarying stages: sensori-motor, preoperational, concrete, and formal, with the latter two of primary importance for college instruction. Concrete learners are limited to manipulating objects and solving problems that are tangible rather than abstract, while formal learners can think in theoretical terms and utilize the complexities of propositional logic to solve problems. Concrete thinkers cannot solve problems requiring assumptions contrary to actual truth, whereas the formal learners can reach conclusions independent of reality (Wadsworth, 1971). For example, the geometry theorem that there exists only one perpendicular from a point to a line can be proved by using the contradiction strategy; that is, by assuming that there are two such lines and then by reaching a logically absurd contradiction during the proof. Students who cannot reason by formal operations cannot make the assumption that there are two such lines, for they know that if they draw a picture, they can draw only one such line. In other words, they cannot suspend reality long enough to let propositional logic work for them to solve the problem. In contrast, the formal thinker has no difficulty making such assumptions and can readily use the contradiction approach.

Movement between stages occurs by a process of self-regulation. When students confront facts contrary to their experience, cognitive disequilibrium is created. This tension becomes the internal motivation to reorganize thinking in order to assimilate new facts into existing thought patterns or to change those patterns. Cognitive development occurs when patterns change. In the example from geometry, disequilibrium occurs when the student sees that truth can be arrived at even on the basis of an absurd assumption (that is, two perpendiculars). On the one hand, students know that there cannot be two perpendiculars. On the other hand they see that the assumption that there are two perpendiculars is a trick of logic and that it works. Hence, a new pattern that suggests reality can be manipulated by using logic. Self-regulation is the process of moving in and out of equilibrium; to the extent that self-regulation can be manipulated, cognitive change occurs.

Karplus (1974) has used the concept of self-regulation to translate Piaget's theory into an instructional strategy to facilitate the development of formal thought. His instructional technique, called the learning cycle, is the basis of ADAPT instruction. The cycle has three phases, exploration, invention, and application, and it takes the student from an observable, tangible, concrete experience to an abstract, formal conclusion.

During the exploration phase, students are confronted with concrete experiences and required to investigate them in an open-ended manner. Through these concrete experiences, the abstract, formal concept of principle can be learned. Students are encouraged to experiment with the concrete experience in as much detail and depth as possible. Information, facts, and data that they have gathered lay the foundation for the creation of disequilibrium and for subsequent change. Next, during the invention stage, the leap is made from the concrete experience to the underlying concept or principle in its abstract or formal nature. The teacher guides the student to the discovery or invention of the concept. Finally, during the application phase, an experience is designed that requires students to apply the concept that they have discovered to new concrete situations. Practice and application firmly establish the new cognitive structure in the student's repertoire.

An example from the ADAPT economics class will clarify the process (Petr, 1977, p. 44). The learning cycle approach is used to teach the concept of consumer price index. As an exploration activity, students compile records of their purchases and prices during a two-week period. No specifications are given for what to buy or in what quantity; students record only their actual purchases.

During the invention stage, students confront the fact that they cannot determine changes in their purchasing power by simply adding up their purchases and comparing the sums between two different time periods, for they do not usually purchase the same goods during different time periods. Thus, the concept of a representative market basket is developed. Students discover how an index of cost must be defined so that it accurately reflects changes in costs from one week to the next. Students quickly discover that not all items bought should be used to compute the index, that items need to be grouped into such categories as food, recreation, and housing, and that the quantity of items purchased should be standardized. Thus, the concrete exploration activity generates data (students' lists of purchases and prices) that in turn create the disequilibrium (noncomparability across time) that is necessary for students to realize that relevant variables must be isolated and methods for handling them in computing the price index must be determined.

Finally, the application exercise asks students to use what they have learned to compare the value of the index at the beginning of each month from one month to the next. Changes in the index provide concrete experience in the measurement of inflation.

This example shows how concrete experience can be manipulated to enhance the learning of formal concepts that would otherwise be beyond the ability of many college students. Problems move students from exploration to invention to application.

Role of the Professor. The professor's role has two separate yet interrelated aspects: designing the course and teaching the course. The primary task in designing an ADAPT course is to create concrete experiences for students to use in the exploration stage of the learning cycle. The concrete experience must not depend on propositional logic or other skills reserved for the formal thinker. For example, in ADAPT physics, students are expected to develop the relationship between mass, period, and amplitude for a harmonic motion system. First, they explore the movement of flexible rods, a vibrating hacksaw blade, and a pendulum. They are asked to investigate the properties of these systems, identify the variables which are present, and find variables that can be controlled. Nothing is expected of the student beyond manipulating and observing concrete laboratory equipment.

ADAPT anthropology provides another example of a concrete experience. Students are asked to discover the rules for saying "hello" to a stranger. During the exploration stage, they pair up to go out and greet people—one student observes and another student greets. Students are expected to only to carry out the assignment and to report their observations to the class. Most students report their observations in units of behavior that are too large—"I said hello, and then she said hello." Careful questioning by the professor leads students to see that other things occur between the two hello's—eye contact, looking away, nervous movements. Thus, the professor begins to create the disequilibrium that is necessary for students to realize that a finer analysis is needed.

The professor's role in teaching an ADAPT course is similar to the role of the professor in a guided design course. The professor is a listener, facilitator, and diagnostician. Listening to students wrestle with problems, allowing students to go their own directions and give their own explanations, is to permit them to think about experiences that are contrary to their own expectations, which creates the necessary state of disequilibrium. Such experience should have far more impact for the student than a correct answer from an authoritative teacher. During the exploratory stage, the professor provides the stimulation that can guide students to new directions and avenues for their consideration.

As a diagnostician, the professor listens to students solve problems and determines the extent to which they have developed their thinking so that further challenges and experiences should be provided. Obviously, this requires the professor to identify those student behaviors that signal formal thought in the problem area at issue. As one ADAPT professor said (Hazen, 1977, p. 106), "the instructor takes on a new role of facilitator of learning activities or even collaborator in the learning activities. He needs to establish a climate of mutual trust, one that is conducive to encouraging the usage of problem-solving and reasoning processes."

Role of the Student. Three attributes define the role of students in the ADAPT program: they must be willing to become active learners and be involved in class; they must be willing to be experimenters; and over the long haul they should become formal operational thinkers.

The view of the student as active learner is similar to Wales's expectation for students in a guided design course, with one addition: class members must be willing to commit themselves to interacting with their environment and their classmates. Both are critical for cognitive change (Piaget, 1952). For example, to talk about the period of a pendulum is necessary but not sufficient for change. Students must also interact with a pendulum, vary the length of its period, try to "push" it to go faster, and conduct other experiments to see what affects its period.

Students must also observe what they have done and then modify the approach and repeat the interaction until a solution is reached. Merely to try something oneself or to watch others try something is insufficient; observation of the result creates disequilibrium if it is not what was anticipated. Modification and subsequent observation are what bring about cognitive change via self-regulation. As one ADAPT professor put it (Peterson, 1977, p. 81), "active participation of the student is required. Without observation and experience, the student will remain at the preconcrete level of operations."

Finally, the student should acquire formal operational reasoning skills—the ability to isolate variables, to manipulate one variable while holding the others constant, and to reason with symbolic logic. It is assumed, at the beginning, that the student does not have these skills. To assist the student to develop formal operational skills, the ADAPT program uses concrete experiences as the basis of the student's interaction with the curriculum. Traditionally, students must supply their own concrete examples of the content under study, because professors usually teach at the abstract or formal level. Students without a wealth of concrete experience to which to relate content feel lost. In the ADAPT program, these concrete experiences are provided, to decrease students' need to recall examples of their own and to increase the applicability of the appropriate concrete experience.

Results. In the course of a single year, ADAPT students improve both their general critical thinking skills and their formal operational reasoning, when compared to other students (Tomlinson-Keasey and Eisert, 1977). Although there remains some question about the design of the research into the program,* the results indicate success in facilitating cognitive change.

Using the Watson-Glaser Critical Thinking Appraisal to assess changes in critical thinking, the ADAPT group improved significantly in critical thinking ability over the course of the year, while the control groups showed little progress (Tomlinson-Keasey and Eisert, 1977, p. 129). Changes in formal operational reasoning were assessed with five tasks that require formal reasoning (Campbell, 1977). When compared to a control group, the ADAPT students showed a substantial increase in formal reasoning (Tomlinson-Keasey and Eisert, 1977, p. 128). Although ADAPT students entered the program with lower test score measures (for example, lower ACT scores) than any of the control sections, they evidenced significant improvement in critical thinking ability as well as movement into formal operational reasoning.

The ADAPT faculty generally find that Piaget's theory is useful in understanding learning problems that they have observed in class. They recognize and accept that many students are not formal thinkers and that a change in the instructional approach is thereby required. Faculty members themselves find the learning cycle "an enjoyable and creative process" (Hazen, 1977, p. 107).

*Control sections were not randomly chosen, and questions remain as to whether appropriate steps were taken in the research design to justify the conclusions that were reached. For example, the formal operational assessment group consisted primarily of sophomores, who on the pretest had a significantly higher level of formal reasoning than the ADAPT group but did not change as much between pretesting and posttesting as the ADAPT group. It is entirely possible that, as freshmen, the control group had a formal operational profile similar to the ADAPT group and also that its members changed as much while they were freshmen. For this reason, the research design is weak, and the results should be interpreted with caution.

Some teachers indicate that students learn the content better using the ADAPT strategy (Petr, 1977, p. 47). According to these teachers, students "have a stronger, surer grasp of what concepts are involved. The ideas mean something to them and are retained and used." Faculty also say that student attitudes toward learning improve with the ADAPT approach. Students show more enthusiasm, they are willing to undertake a greater amount of work, and they are responsible for their own learning. One ADAPT teacher summed it up in these words (Duly, 1977, p. 63): "If Piaget has a particular significance for the teacher . . . , it is that it transfers to the student responsibility for learning. It decreases passivity. And it allows even first semester students to discover that the pleasures of the discipline can be shared by them."

Summary. The ADAPT approach to instruction in problem solving emphasizes changes in students' cognitive strategies. Professors are listeners, facilitators, and diagnosticians, while students are active learners who experiment with and manipulate their environment to develop as formal thinkers. Analysis of the ADAPT curriculum indicates that students become formal operational thinkers and better critical thinkers. Faculty find that the curriculum is an excellent device for engaging students in their own learning and development.

Rubinstein's "Patterns of Problem Solving"

In contrast to guided design and the ADAPT program, which emphasize problem solving processes and developmental activities, Rubinstein's approach to problem solving emphasizes content. He focuses on *content* that is prerequisite for mathematical, scientific, or engineering problem solving, "the tools and concepts which are most productive to problem solving" (Rubinstein, 1975, p. xiii).

Strategy Description. Rubinstein's basic assumption about problem solving is that there are certain areas of content that problem solvers must master to be successful. These areas provide techniques for reducing uncertainty in problem solving. Rubinstein's course text, *Patterns of Problem Solving* (1975), presents numerous content areas, including probability and probability models, modeling theory, decision-making theory, and optimization strategies.

Each strategy takes a fairly sophisticated mathematical approach that occasionally requires knowledge of the calculus. Although rigor and theory are stressed, each content area presents a unified approach for decreasing uncertainty when making problem solving decisions. For example, the chapter on probability theory explains how application of that content reduces uncertainty in problem solving. The central focus of this chapter is the question, "When is doubt low enough so that a 'reasonable' decision can be made about a set of data?" Background information on the quantitative nature of probability, the mathematical formulae used to compute probabilities under different conditions, and the theoretical and mathematical background of probability models is presented. The chapter includes a rigorous mathematical treatment of probability, so that students develop the ability to make complex decisions involving probability approaches to problem solving.

One example will serve to illustrate the kinds of real-world problem solving that students are capable of after studying the chapter on probability. Students are asked to determine when the uncertainty of the information from a diagnostic test for cancer is low enough that an appropriate diagnosis can be made. They are given the probabilities of a false positive and false negative diagnosis (that is, diagnosis of cancer when it is not present and no diagnosing of cancer when it is present). They are also given data on the proportion of the general population that has cancer. Then, students are directed to compute the probability that a randomly selected person has cancer and, given a negative diagnosis, that the same person does not have cancer. Professionals face such problems every day. These patterns show students that much in problem solving is not "exact" science, but that an element of uncertainty is involved. However, students learn that there are techniques available to the problem solver which can reduce the uncertainty to acceptable limits.

Once a firm foundation in probability has been established, Rubinstein's text considers some statistical approaches to problem solving. The normal curve and the concepts of mean and variance are introduced. These topics lead to a discussion of elementary research design for determining whether given characteristics are significant for selected samples of items. Such concepts as sample size, z-statistic, the central limit theorem, hypothesis testing models, and type I and type II errors are discussed. Although calculus concepts are used to present the theoretical content, students should nevertheless be able to design a simple research experiment, gather the data, analyze them and make appropriate inferences to the population. Thus, the addition of statistical strategies to the student's repertoire adds further techniques for the reduction of doubt in decision making.

When students have mastered these basic statistical concepts, simple research-type problems can be solved. For example, given the mean and variance of a certain population for the failure rate of the U-joint in a 1975 Oldsmobile, the engineering student is now equipped to determine whether the mean failure rate computed for the sample under consideration is significantly different from that for the original population. Solving such problems involves use of the z-statistic, construction of appropriate hypothesis testing models, and determination of the conditions under which results are significant.

Role of the Professor. It is difficult to describe the role of either the professor or the student under Rubinstein's approach because it depends upon the instructional strategy that is used, and this can vary from instructor to instructor. The challenge to the professor is to develop an instructional approach that facilitates student learning of complex and rigorous content. The professor must decide what mathematical prerequisites will be required, whether the theoretical approach exemplified by the text or a neomathematical approach will be followed, and whether the course will be offered only to certain majors or will be broader in its applications to many majors.

The professor must also decide whether formal operational thinking, as in the ADAPT program, is needed for successful completion of the course. If the professor determines that it is necessary, then techniques need to be used to facilitate cognitive development of students taking the course or a screening process must be developed to sift out the preformal thinker. ADAPT's exploration, invention, and application instructional sequence would be useful here.

Role of the Student. As in the case of the professor, the student's role is unclear until a particular instructional strategy has been decided upon. If the course is taught from the rigorous mathematical approach used in the text, the student must have a good background in mathematics, including beginning calculus. However, the content can also be taught with less mathematical sophistication, so that it requires less mathematical background of the students. Similarly, formal operational reasoning would be required if the course is taught at the sophisticated level of the text, but a less rigorous approach could also be adopted for concrete operational learners.

Results. The particular content that Rubinstein covers has yet to be studied for its impact on problem-solving behavior. A number of approaches could be used to validate the usefulness of this content for certain types of problem solving. First, the opinions of professional engineers, mathematicians, and scientists could be gathered to determine whether they use this content when they solve problems. Second, a strict behavioral task analysis could be conducted to determine whether the Rubinstein content is appropriate for problems requiring techniques that reduce uncertainty. Ultimately, if outcome behaviors could be specified for the type of problem solving required, then a detailed study involving actual performance could be carried out to determine the effectiveness of this approach as compared to others. In addition, data similar to those which Wales reports to document the effectiveness of guided design could be gathered and analyzed to determine whether Rubinstein's approach made any impact on attrition or grade point averages.

Remedial and Developmental Education

Some students seem to know that they cannot learn what you have to teach them. They may come to class or they may not, but you know for sure that they have no idea of what you are talking about. In fact, you wonder how they sat through so many hours of schooling without absorbing anything. If you schedule an office hour with them, they may appear or they may find that some other problem prevents them from seeing you. If they do show, they don't seem to know how to talk to you. You already know that they don't know how to listen, that they don't take notes, and that they never contribute to class discussion. But what is worse is that you don't know how to talk to them.

Clearly, these students lack basic survival skills for a university education. You, too, may lack either the skills or the time to offer such students adequate assistance. Increasingly, remedial or developmental programs are assisting this type of student.

On the preceding pages, we have described some ways of improving problem-solving instruction that focus on process, cognitive prerequisites, and content. In the following paragraphs, the role of remedial education is discussed, especially its emphasis on the development of a positive academic self-concept and of an attitude about learning that is oriented to success, rather than failure. A positive self-concept and a success-oriented attitude are essential elements in successful problem solving and critical thinking.

Strategy Description. In their assessment of remedial education programs, Roueche and others propose that the building of a "cycle of success" should be the basic strategy in developing success-oriented self-concept (Roueche and Pitman, 1972; Roueche and Kirk, 1973; Roueche, 1976; Roueche and Mink, 1976a, 1976b; Roueche and Snow, 1977). Institutional strategies, counseling approaches, and peer intervention techniques have been outlined, but I want here to focus only on instructional strategies that facilitate the cycle of success. Roueche indicates that systematic design of instruction, individualized teaching and learning strategies, criterion-referenced evaluation, and teacher behaviors that communicate caring and expectations for success are four strategies that facilitate building the cycle that promotes learning and thinking on the part of students.

Systematic design of instruction means that there is "congruence among objectives, teaching strategy, and evaluation of student performance" (Briggs, 1977, p. 5). Usually, this goal requires behaviorally stated objectives, pretests for prerequisite knowledge, instruction for prerequisites not yet mastered, and a variety of learning options and approaches to master stated course objectives. A well-designed unit of teaching organizes learning for students so that students know what they are to learn and have strategies available for learning this and then for knowing how well they learned it. Recently, I worked with a professor of English who was developing a remedial English course for students. Her efforts to design her instruction systematically extended over more than three years and encompassed such alternatives as computer-assisted testing, self-instructional packages, and a sophisticated self-paced instructional method. When I joined her, she had begun work on the very careful—and sometimes painful—process of committing to paper exactly what she wanted her students to be able to do when they finished her course. In short, she was specifying learning objectives for her students.

When that had been completed, she was in a position to consider how and what to pretest, because her students came into the course with a wide range of knowledge. Her pretest went through a number of revisions and now it provides precise information on student entry abilities. After taking the pretest, students receive a computer printout listing the questions missed, the relevant course objective, and a strategy for learning what they need to know. Through this system of diagnosis and prescription, the professor has a high degree of effect on her students and what they will learn.

The second approach toward building a cycle of success involves the use of individualized instruction. An individualized curriculum allows students to begin study of the content at whatever level they enter and to proceed at their own pace and it provides alternative methods and materials for achieving its objectives. Roueche and Snow (1977, p. 117) suggest that individualized instruction ensures that "learning is geared to present capabilities of each student."

Individualized systems often require students to master concepts before they move on to others. Students who fail to reach mastery of the material return to additional learning experiences before being retested. Although a mastery, self-paced individualized system can be complex and difficult to design and administer, it has great potential for helping to create the success cycle for students. Cross (1976, p. 78) believes that "mastery learning is the critical missing link in the education of low achievers" not only because it lays a firm foundation for future learning but also because it shows the failure-oriented students that they can learn.

The English professor who developed the remedial course utilized a mastery, self-paced system which individualized instruction to the needs of each student. After studying a unit of material and taking a posttest on the material, learners who failed to reach the mastery level were returned to additional material on the same topics. Interestingly, the professor found that her students completed significantly more units than students in a comparable section taught with the traditional lecture-discussion method (Moss and Stonewater, 1980).

A third strategy for effecting more positive attitudes toward problem solving focuses on the way in which rewards and success are related to individual students. Learners' performances might best be judged, graded, or rated against standard pre-established criteria, using criterion-referenced evaluation systems rather than norm-referenced systems. Relating students' achievements to an outside, objective standard rather than to the work of other students helps students to see that their own actions determine rewards in learning and thinking.

The last strategy for stimulating successful thinking concerns the manner in which professors relate to students in the classroom. Teachers can communicate caring and expectations for success verbally and through their behavior. For example, by their words teachers can indicate their concern that each student should understand the lecture, and to indicate this concern in behavior they can involve the less confident students in class activities. Teacher expectations of student performance is one of the most critical variables in students' actual performance (Rosenthal and Jacobson, 1968). The professor who expects all students to know the answers to his or her questions communicates a success orientation.

I usually discuss my intentions with my class. If its members know that I will call on them because I want them to learn, they are more likely to respond in a way constructive to their learning. Another strategy that I use to communicate my concern is to ask the students for feedback about me and the class early in the semester. When I first tried this technique, I was amazed at how it affected my class. It was evident that students felt that I cared about what they learned, how they learned it, and how I affected them. Besides being easy to use, this device also provides me with much valuable information on my performance in facilitating students' learning and thinking.

How do systematically designed instruction, individualized strategies, criterion-referenced feedback, and caring attitudes fit together to enhance student success? In a single phrase, they consider the total student; that is the important ingredient. Unless we care about students and know what makes them tick, we cannot really teach them anything. Unless we listen and hear what students are telling us, both verbally and nonverbally, we cannot be sure that what we are telling them is being received as we intend.

Role of the Professor. When confronted with the need for systematically designed instruction, individualized learning approaches, criterion-referenced evaluation systems, and response to students in caring and success-oriented ways, many professors are being asked to use new skills to address unfamiliar ideas. The teacher must become an educational specialist and learning consultant, well-versed in learning theory and the latest instructional development theory and techniques. The teacher must be aware of what others have tried to do and of their successes and failures. Although many campuses have professionals who assist with development of new types of instruction and with planning for new systems of evaluation, the job remains the professor's.

The professor may also be asked to develop new ways of relating to students. Most of us already care about our students' learnng, but we can always improve our techniques for communicating this caring to them. As I have indicated, simply asking your class for feedback does a lot to establish a caring environment. Taking time to paraphrase a student's remark or question communicates not only that you are concerned about understanding what the student says but also that you care enough to take a little extra time to hear the student accurately. You need only remember the last time that you asked a question yourself and found that the response indicated that the question had not been accurately heard.

On a somewhat more sophisticated level, we can develop an awareness of the behaviors and language that we use in the classroom to ensure that they do not communicate subtle messages that reinforce the negative self-concept and failure-oriented worlds of remedial students. Videotaping a lecture or two can provide surprising insight into how we present ourselves to our classes. We must also be clear about our own needs as professionals. Some of us are not likely to succeed in the remedial classroom, regardless of the techniques that we may think we know. The research-oriented professor who likes to give a lecture, hold office hours, and return to the lab is unlikely to be successful in teaching problem solving and critical thinking skills to remedial students, regardless of the assistance that is available.

For many professors, involvement in a remedial program requires a change in philosophy about the nature of a university education and the role of the teacher. Roueche and Snow (1977, p. 118) well summarize the professor's role: "We should emphasize here that the form of instruction (methodology and the like) may not be as important as the students' perceptions of the teacher's behavior and their perception that the teacher is endeavoring to help students succeed. A teacher willing to develop materials, specify objectives, and accommodate individual differences is simply showing his students that he is willing to make learning possible."

Role of the Student. The strategies that have been described here tend to view the student as one who is acted upon. Courses are designed in particular ways and professors must respond to students in certain ways. Although much can be said for strategies that attempt to manipulate the environment to increase the probability of students' successful interaction with it, there are things that students can do themselves to ensure success. First, students can learn that they are in control of what happens to them. If a professor responds in uncaring or failure-oriented ways, the student must learn not to respond with failure-oriented behaviors. The remedial student who encounters a professor who states, "Twenty percent of this class usually fails" must learn to say, "Not me" instead of giving up. The student who has been sick for a week and sees that it is almost impossible to catch up on everything must learn to outline a plan of action for catching up: "I'll give it a try by seeing my professors and asking for help, I'll go the the help session, and I will spend an extra hour in the morning in the library." It is critical for the remedial student to develop skills for taking control of what happens.

Results. Bloom (1978) argues that as many as 95 percent of today's students can learn anything, given sufficient time to learn it. Clearly, he implies that most remedial students can learn college-level material to a mastery level, given sufficient time to learn. Individualized courses for high-risk remedial students result in better retention and achievement and in perceptions that they can succeed in college (Roueche and Mink, 1976b). This research also shows a dramatic increase in students' feelings of self-control after exposure to individualized instruction. This is an essential characteristic for effective learning and thinking. Other studies show that communicating objectives to remedial students enhances their achievement (Cross, 1971) and that students perform to superior levels when a self-paced, mastery requirement is placed on individualized learning (Kulik, Kulik, and Smith, 1976). Finally, still other evidence indicates that involvement with students in a caring, supportive environment can increase retention. At Santa Fe Community College at Gainesville, Florida, students are visited by a peer counselor and a teacher after their first absence from class. The retention rate at this college is 90 percent.

Summary. Remedial programs are viewed here as educational experiences designed to help students develop positive academic self-concepts and success-oriented attitudes toward learning, especially toward learning for problem solving. Strategies appropriate for remedial programs are focused on systematically designed instruction, individualized instruction, individualized courses, criterion-referenced evaluation, and response to students in caring and success-oriented ways. Professors must develop new skills as instructional experts and they must practice ways of communicating their concerns for student learning and success to students. For their part, students need to become involved in the curriculum so that they can feel more in control of their environment.

Successful Teaching for Problem Solving

I have discussed the essentials of four approaches to the teaching of problem solving. What remains to be done is to synthesize what I see to be the most fundamental and important components of effective problem solving instruction. Each strategy that has been discussed brings about fundamental changes in student capabilities and provides students with new tools that can be utilized in lifelong learning. If each strategy used by itself brings success, then an eclectic combination of all four may produce even better results. I would like first to summarize these strategies and then to present the big picture from my vantage point of the things that professors can do to help their students learn to be better problem solvers.

Problem Solving Strategies. Each problem solving strategy emphasizes different goals for the learner and different ways of reaching them. In guided design, students learn to transfer the procedure for problem solving to any setting; hence, the student possesses a new tool by which to continue learning. The end product of the ADAPT program is a change in student thinking abilities that in turn makes advanced learning possible. Rubinstein's approach provides students with content that they can build upon and utilize for further learning. As the outcome of remedial programs, students view learning as something that they can accomplish and that they can be in control of.

Further, each strategy takes a different view of the role of the learner. The guided design student is actively involved in the course, applying the process to solve problems and learning course content independently of the professor. Similarly, the ADAPT student is involved in experimenting with the learning cycle activities to bridge the gap between concrete and formal reasoning. In contrast, the emphasis of Rubinstein's work is that the student is cognitively mature and probably learns well by "receiving" information from the teacher. Remedial programs evidence yet another view of the learner as one whose environment must be shaped and molded to create the highest probability that the student will interact with it in a positive and successful way.

In each of the four problem solving approaches, the professor is called upon to perform certain tasks. The guided design professor must design the course by identifying problems around which to build the content. The ADAPT professor must identify concrete examples that lead to the development of a formal operational understanding of abstract content. The professor who uses Rubinstein's text is called upon to make decisions about the mathematical prerequisites that can be assumed and about whether to follow the theoretical approach of the text. Finally, planners of remedial programs must systematically design individualized courses that are in tune with students' learning needs and styles.

The ADAPT and guided design professors both are supporters of a process rather than disseminators of content. The role of the professor is to ask questions that stimulate thinking and provide direction, give feedback in a supportive manner, and help students to draw their own conclusions. The professor who uses Rubinstein's text leans toward the traditional lecturer's role. The remedial professor resembles the ADAPT and guided design instructors, especially by the charge to communicate caring and success attitudes to students.

Thus, these four strategies differ in their end goals, in how they attempt to accomplish these goals, in their views of the professors' role, and in their expectations for how students should behave and change as a result of instruction.

Components of Success. Five components of effective problem solving instruction emerge from the research on these four strategies and my own experience with the teaching and learning process. When I consult with a professor who believes that problem solving is teachable and who wants to address problem solving instruction, I recommend that the professor do five things: listen to Piaget—his theory on how the concrete learner leaves the world of what he or she can see, hear, and manipulate to move into a world of abstractions, logic, and assumptions is absolutely critical for developing instruction for problem solving; insist on mastery learning of content or process, but allow learners to get there in their own time—self-paced, mastery learning works because it ensures that the foundation is there for the things that come after; pay attention to the design of instruction—the learning goals that a teacher sets and the methods used to achieve them have an effect on student performance; give students feedback on the many little details that go into problem solving as well as on their success in producing an acceptable solution; and encourage group learning—two problem solvers are better than one.

The development of formal operational thinking is critical to successful problem solving. Piaget's approach is the basis of the ADAPT program, in which specifc instructional strategies are developed to help students move into formal thought. The approach used in developing concrete-based experiences for the nonformal reasoner has been shown to be an effective technique for facilitating formal thought development (McKinnon, 1970; Renner and Lawson, 1975). The assumption that many college students have not reached the formal operational level is well documented (Elkind, 1962; Griffiths, 1973; McKinnon, 1970; Stonewater, 1977; Tower and Wheatley, 1971).

Piaget is right. Let me tell a little story to illustrate this point. I conduct research using Piaget's ideas, I develop problem solving courses based on Piaget's principles, and I generally expound his virtues. His theory always worked in the laboratory with students. One morning, I was sitting at the breakfast table with my four-year-old, and she had two glasses of equal volume but different height at her place. I asked her a classic Piaget question: What would happen if she poured her orange juice from the shorter glass, which is full, into the taller glass, which is empty? A four-year-old is supposed to tell you that the taller glass will have more orange juice in it after pouring; she cannot yet comprehend that size and shape of containers make no difference to the quantity inside them, and this is the answer she gave me. Nevertheless, I was amazed to see that the theory works. I tell this little story to reinforce my assertion that Piaget really knows what he is talking about. The concrete thinker is not capable of the rigors required for effective problem solving. You as the teacher must deal with this fact.

Next, the self-paced mastery instructional approach provides an effective way of teaching for problem solving. Both guided design and successful remedial programs take this approach. In guided design, students work in groups at their own speed to solve problems which must pass the professor's criteria of mastery before they can proceed. The individualized courses recommended for remedial programs include self-paced mastery conditions. In their survey of self-paced instruction, Kulik, Kulik, and Smith (1976) report that in thirty-four out of thirty-nine studies, the self-paced section was statistically superior in final exam performance than the traditional lecture-discussion section. Success occurs because students have the opportunity to take as long as they need to learn the content, because they are responsible for their own learning, and because they are actively involved in their learning, not passive receivers of information. Different people learn at different rates, and if an individual fails to learn a given topic, every topic that depends on it becomes unlearnable. If students do not learn how to identify the unknown in a problem or how to specify the problem to be solved, then subsequent problem solving that requires these skills is nearly impossible. Individual differences in learning rate and the need to master prerequisite material are two facts that you as the professor must deal with. Self-paced mastery instruction is a solution.

Emphasis on the systematic design of instruction is the third critical component for effective problem solving instruction. Roueche and Snow (1977) point out that this element is especially important in effective remedial programs. Systematic design of instruction leads to improved performance on the part of the student, especially the less capable student. Bloom (1976, p. 134) points out that "more mature and capable learners will be least influenced by varying qualities of instruction, while less mature or less capable learners will be most influenced by quality of instruction."

The fourth critical feaure of effective problem solving instruction is feedback to students. Guided design provides feedback by the professor's comments to students after each step in the process. In remedial programs, feedback is an essential part of individualized instruction (Roueche and Snow, 1977). In the ADAPT program, students receive much of their feedback from the activities that they experiment with in the learning cycle. The very nature of the self-regulation process and the creation of disequilibrium is based on feedback from action taken by the student. The educational literature and experiences both clearly indicate the central role of feedback in instruction. Bloom (1978, p. 566) indicates that regular corrective feedback will make the individual learning rates of students in a group more similar by reducing the number of slow learners. Gilbert's (1978) research substantiates the approach. According to this author (p. 179), "we have invariably been able to achieve a substantial improvement in measured performance—never less than a 20 percent improvement, often a 50 percent change, and sometimes improvements as high as sixfold" when corrective feedback is used.

The final component of successful problem solving instruction is the use of group learning. Guided design work is accomplished entirely in groups, and much of the experimenting in the ADAPT program is done in groups in order to maximize ideas and input. The research suggests that group problem solving performance is superior to individual performance because a group can bring more strategies to bear on the solution, remember more information, propose more alternative solutions, and verify solutions more readily (Klausmeier and Goodwin, 1966, p. 271). When the professor's feedback is added, the responses that a group of students can produce far exceed those available to a single individual acting alone.

We as teachers can be aware of the strategies that facilitate the development of thinking from the concrete to formal stage, that allow for individual differences in learning and ensure mastery, that facilitate systematically designed instruction, that provide feedback to students, and that encourage group learning. Again, I reflect upon the student in my class who said, "Aha—I see it now," and again I ask whether the "aha" was the result of divine intervention, luck, or my teaching. I would be better justified in concluding that it had been my teaching if I had used some of the ideas and techniques suggested by Wales, ADAPT, Rubinstein, and Roueche. No one approach says it all, but all four, taken together, provide a solid foundation for further consideration of a more sophisticated, eclectic, and broad-based approach to the teaching and learning of problem solving.

References

Bloom, B. S. *Human Characteristics and School Learning.* New York: McGraw-Hill, 1976.

Bloom, B. S. "New Views of the Learner: Implications for Instruction and Curriculum." *Educational Leadership,* 1978, *35* (7), 563–576.

Briggs, L. J. "Introduction." In L. J. Briggs (Ed.), *Instructional Design: Principles and Applications.* Englewood Cliffs, N.J.: Educational Technology Publications, 1977.

Campbell, T. C. "An Evaluation of a Learning Cycle Intervention Strategy for Enhancing the Use of Formal Operational Thought by Beginning College Physics Students." Unpublished doctoral dissertation, University of Nebraska, 1977.

Cross, K. P. *Beyond the Open Door: New Students in Higher Education.* San Francisco: Jossey-Bass, 1971.

Cross, K. P. *Accent on Learning: Improving Instruction and Reshaping the Curriculum.* San Francisco: Jossey-Bass, 1976.

Duly, L. C. "ADAPT History." In R. G. Fuller (Ed.), *Multidisciplinary Piagetian-Based Programs for College Freshmen.* Lincoln: University of Nebraska, 1977.

Elkind, D. "Quantity Concepts in College Students." *Journal of Social Psychology,* 1962, *57,* 459-465.

Fuller, R. G. (Ed.). *Multidisciplinary Piaetian-Based Programs for College Freshmen.* Lincoln: University of Nebraska, 1977.

Gilbert, T. F. *Human Competence: Engineering Worthy Performance.* New York: McGraw-Hill, 1978.

Griffiths, D. H. "The Study of the Cognitive Development of Science Students in Introductory Level Courses." Unpublished doctoral dissertation, Rutgers University, 1973.

Hazen, M. V. H. "The Impact of the ADAPT Programs on the Teaching of Data Processing." In R. G. Fuller (Ed.), *Multidisciplinary Piagetian-Based Programs for College Freshmen.* Lincoln: University of Nebraska, 1977.

Karplus, R. *Science Curriculum Improvement Study: Teacher's Handbook.* Berkeley, Calif.: Lawrence Hall of Science, 1974.

Klausmeier, H. J., and Goodwin, W. *Learning and Human Abilities.* New York: Harper & Row, 1966.

Kulik, J. A., Kulik, C. C., and Smith, B. B. "Research on the Personalized System of Instruction." *Programmed Learning and Educational Technology,* 1976, *13,* 23-30.

McKinnon, J. W. "The Influence of a College Inquiry-Centered Course in Science on Student Entry into the Formal Operational Stage." Unpublished doctoral dissertation, University of Oklahoma, 1970.

Moss, C., and Stonewater, J. K. "Performance of Special-Admissions Students in Basic Writing Courses: Instructor-Pacing Versus Self-Pacing." Unpublished manuscript, 1980.

Peterson, M. Q. "ADAPT Anthro." In R. G. Fuller (Ed.), *Multidisciplinary Piagetian-Based Programs for College Freshmen.* Lincoln: University of Nebraska, 1977.

Petr, J. L. "Piaget and Learning Economics." In R. G. Fuller (Ed.), *Multidisciplinary Piagetian-Based Programs for College Freshmen.* Lincoln: University of Nebraska, 1977.

Piaget, J. *Judgment and Reasoning in the Child.* New York: Humanities Press, 1952.

Renner, J. W., and Lawson, A. E. "Intellectual Development in Preservice Elementary School Teachers: An Evaluation." *Journal of College Science Teaching,* 1975, *5* (2), 89-92.

Rosenthal, R., and Jacobson, T. *Pygmalion in the Classroom.* New York: Holt, Rinehart and Winston, 1968.

Roueche, J. E. "Creating an Environment for Learning." *Community and Junior College Journal,* 1976, *46,* 48-50.

Roueche, J. E., and Kirk, R. W. *Catching Up: Remedial Education.* San Francisco: Jossey-Bass, 1973.

Roueche, J. E., and Mink, O. G. "Helping the 'Unmotivated' Student: Toward Personhood Development." *Community College Review,* 1976a, *3* (4), 40-50.

Roueche, J. E., and Mink, O. G. *The Impact of Instruction and Counseling on High Risk Youth: Final Report.* Austin, Tex.: Community College Leadership Program, 1976b.

Roueche, J. E., and Pitman, J. C. *A Modest Proposal: Students Can Learn.* San Francisco: Jossey-Bass, 1972.

Roueche, J. E., and Snow, J. J. *Overcoming Learning Problems: A Guide to Developmental Education in College.* San Francisco: Jossey-Bass, 1977.

Rubinstein, M. F. *Patterns of Problem Solving.* Englewood Cliffs, N.J.: Prentice-Hall, 1975.

Stonewater, J. K. "Instruction in Problem Solving and Piaget's Theory of Cognitive Development." Unpublished doctoral dissertation, Michigan State University, 1977.

Tomlinson-Keasey, C. A., and Eisert, D. "Second Year Evaluation of the ADAPT Program." In R. G. Fuller (Ed.), *Multidisciplinary Piagetian-Based Programs for College Freshmen.* Lincoln: University of Nebraska, 1977.

Tower, J. O., and Wheatley, G. "Conservation Concepts in College Students: A Replication and Critique." *Journal of Genetic Psychology,* 1971, *118,* 265–270.

Tseng, M. S., and Wales, C. E. "Effect of a Guided Design Course Pattern on Student Personality Variables." *Engineering Education,* 1972, *62,* 812–813.

Wadsworth, B. J. *Piaget's Theory of Cognitive Development.* New York: McKay, 1971.

Wales, C. E., and Stager, R. A. *Guided Design, Part I.* Morgantown: West Virginia University, 1977.

Wales, C. E., Stager, R. A., and Long, T. R. *Guided Engineering Design Project Book.* St. Paul, Minn.: West, 1974.

Jerry K. Stonewater is assistant professor of instructional development at Southern Illinois University at Carbondale, where he consults with faculty about strategies for improving the teaching and learning environment. He has designed approaches to teaching problem solving and has studied their effects on the cognitive development of college students

Tackling critical thinking in the context of an actual course is a source of problems and pleasures to all participants.

Critical Thinking: Some Views from the Front Line

Marilla D. Svinicki
Richard H. Kraemer

What is it like to participate in a course which tries to foster critical thinking? According to one student, "The emphasis on critical thinking *makes* this course. Without critical thinking, college is an exercise in endurance rather than education." From the point of view of the instructor, "In teaching contemporary, controversial, and complex material and in doing it with obvious commitment, we overcame the criticisms levelled at the orthodox courses. And we did much more. We discovered new facets of ourselves, our students, and our disciplines." Finally, as one teaching assistant put it, "Being a TA in 'The American Experience' is a mixed blessing. We have a lot of say in what happens, but we also have a lot of responsibility. When a group is going well, it's fantastic. But when a group is bad, it's the worst."

The authors would like to thank the GS610 teaching assistants, Alan Kamasaki, Abelardo Garza, Vincent Shepherd, and Gail Watkins, for providing us with their own reactions and for their assistance in obtaining reactions from students. The authors would also like to thank Professor Thomas L. Philpott of the Department of History, the team teacher in GS610—a superb teacher with enormous commitment and a unique ability to destroy complacency and make people think.

When it comes to teaching, theory and reality seem to be quite different things. This chapter deals with reality, the reality of teaching critical thinking. Sooner or later, mere mortals must translate theorizing into the everyday necessities of the classroom. How do they do it? How do they feel about it? What joys and sorrows do they experience during the process? We asked these questions of real people involved in the teaching and learning of critical thinking in one course.

Critical Thinking and the American Experience

In interviews and written evaluations, we posed questions about life in this course to all those involved or concerned: students, instructors, teaching assistants, and administrators. We used their responses to paint a picture of what participation in such a course means. The course is entitled "The American Experience." It is team taught by faculty from the government and history departments at the University of Texas at Austin and is offered as an alternative to three-hour sections of government and history taught independently by these two departments. In spite of its required status and its typical enrollment of up to 500 students per semester, this course has become one of the most popular at the University since it was first offered in 1970. More relevant to our purposes, the development of critical thinking is one of its main goals.

One Instructor's View*

I have been one of the instructors in this course every semester since it started, so I can speak authoritatively on the highs and lows of trying to teach critical thinking under these conditions.

I find that working with this course gives me a tremendous amount of satisfaction. It gives me the opportunity to do something important with a lot of students, close to 1,100 each year. If we can convince even 50 percent of the class to start applying the processes of critical thinking to their decision making, we will have accomplished something. I grant that the administration of this course (for which I am responsible) is very time-consuming and burdensome, but I am willing to pay that price because I feel that we have the opportunity to start these students off on the right foot, so that they do not waste their college years uncritically accepting everything they hear.

This course grew out of the student movement of the 1960s. Students protested against orthodox college courses in general and against large, required introductory courses in particular. The complaint was

*Richard H. Kraemer.

that such courses were dull, irrelevant, and impersonal and that teachers were often poorly motivated, remote, and "superior" to the students. In many cases, especially on campuses where the incentive system rewards research and publication and largely ignores teaching, the students were right. John Silber, then the highly active dean of our College of Arts and Sciences, listened to the criticisms about such courses and relayed them to department heads to no effect. Finally, he obtained a grant from a foundation and offered financial support to faculty members who would volunteer to design innovative introductory courses. Six were funded, but only one, "The American Experience," survived.

Initially, we did not set out to teach critical thinking. We set out to design a course that would convey the excitement we felt for American history and politics to students. We set out to satisfy the critics—to design a course that students would not find dull, irrelevant, or impersonal but the opposite. We abandoned most conventional approaches to American history and government. Instead, we chose six topics that we felt to be highly important, relevant, and controversial and that gave us an opportunity to say important things about American history and politics. The six original topics were leadership, war and peace, race, urban America, the individual society, and change and the American character. In ten years, some of the titles and sequencing have changed, but the topics remain basically the same.

In teaching contemporary, controversial, and complex material and in doing it with obvious commitment, we overcame the criticisms levelled at the orthodox courses. And we did much more. We discovered new facets of ourselves, our students, and our disciplines.

We also discovered that orthodox test questions were inappropriate. The recitation of facts did not interest us. We felt that the important thing was to determine if students could use the facts to develop and support an intelligent, rational, and enlightened position on controversial areas and issues. We wanted them not only to know some facts but, more important, to go beyond the facts to the intellectual activities that lead to wisdom. In short, we wanted to develop critical thinkers.

On the first day of class, I begin by sharing two quotations—"If a way to the better there be, it lies in taking a good look at the worst" (Thomas Hardy) and "Men who create power make an indispensable contribution to the nation's greatness, but the men who question power make a contribution just as indispensable" (John F. Kennedy). This does two things. It lets the students know that this is a different kind of course, questioning and critical. And it also legitimizes the approach. They do not know who Hardy is until I tell them, but they do know Kennedy and respect him. They also encounter these two quotes in two texts used in the course.

Next, I tell them that we are very concerned about their ability to read and write and that we are going to try to help them improve their reading and writing. Why? Because words are among the most important symbols that we use in thinking, and because learning to think clearly, objectively, critically is what college is all about.

My approach is very simple. It is highly consistent with what our political leaders tell us on the Fourth of July. I am a Jeffersonian democrat and I tell them so. I believe in the Jeffersonian model of the American citizen, who is interested in public policy, active in public policy decision making, and educated enough to understand the issues and to act rationally on his or her own behalf. Anything less than that results in a corruption of democracy. The critical thinker, then, is an independent thinker capable of seeing clearly, thinking objectively, and acting wisely on his or her own behalf.

We use a number of ways to encourage critical thinking. First, I give each of the teaching assistants a copy of Bloom (1956) and a copy of Krathwohl and others (1964). Bloom lays out intellectual activity on six levels. From the lowest to the highest in complexity, these six levels are knowledge, comprehension, application, analysis, synthesis, and evaluation. Bloom's taxonomy provides key words and concepts for dealing with each of these levels. Frequently, the discussion leaders pass on the taxonomy intact to their students. In any case, most of the discussion leaders enjoy working at the upper levels of the taxonomy, and the discussions they lead—such as discussions in which students analyze their own political socialization, which are clearly pitched at the analysis level—and the topics they assign for student papers—such as the evaluation of city service levels in different neighborhoods of Austin and the way they reflect on political power, which requires both analysis and evaluation—illustrate the intent of assistants and instructors to teach critical thinking. These higher-level activities are the essence of critical thinking.

Second, we teach largely, though not exclusively, through works of fiction and biography rather than texts. Such books as *Native Son, Black Elk Speaks, Hard Living on Clay Street,* and *Killers of the Dream* (Smith, 1969) are on our current reading list. We are convinced that the use of such books as these reduces the students' tendency to memorize and increases the tendency to understand and to become involved, at least vicariously.

We also guide the students' thinking and preparation for examinations by distributing, two weeks in advance, study guides for the midterm and final examinations. The examinations are taken entirely from the study guides. There are no surprises. We think that students are entitled to know beforehand exactly what and how much is expected.

We use only essay questions, and rather long and complex ones at that. One question in a recent final examination described Aristotle's concept of justice as given in Book Five of the *Nichomachean Ethics* and then asked students to choose two groups from among blacks, women, blue-collar workers, Chicanos, American Indians and white immigrants; describe "the American experience" of those groups; determine whether they had been treated justly; and, if they had not, propose a proper Aristotelian remedy. Further, students also had to evaluate the applicability of Aristotle's concept of justice to American society. Clearly, this involved analysis, synthesis, and evaluation as defined by Bloom (1956).

A question of this sort cannot be answered by the mere repetition of facts, because there is no "factual" answer to the question of what is just or whether Aristotle's justice applies to modern American society. The student must go beyond facts, search out the relevant ideas, formulate an opinion, and support it with information gleaned from readings and lectures. Since students know long beforehand what type of question they will be asked, they can spend their study time developing relevant arguments and searching out supporting details. This strategy forces them to engage in what we consider to be critical thinking.

Can students in an introductory course handle such questions? The majority have considerable difficulty at first, but, after a midterm, two papers, and a final examination that all require analysis, synthesis, and evaluation, the great majority show substantial improvement and many perform very well. In the process, they seem also to develop pride and confidence in their achievement, and this stimulates their intellectual appetite. In fall 1979, when asked if she was ready for the final exam, one student responded, "I wish I could write on all six questions. [They were required to write on only two.] They are all interesting and important questions, and I want to be able to express myself on all of them."

Of course, there are problems with a course such as this. Administration is more difficult. Getting the right multimedia auditorium and scheduling twenty-four discussion sections takes time and careful planning. We operate democratically (Jefferson would have been proud of us), so it is difficult and time-consuming to bring together two instructors and eight to ten graduate student discussion leaders from two different departments for syllabus preparation, text selection, exam writing, and the discussion of grading, academic dishonesty, and other matters. Giving everyone a chance to speak and arriving at a consensus without alienating anyone take time and patience and skill. The difficulty is increased by the focus of the course on critical thinking. Everyone brings to the course his or her own conceptualization and bias about critical thinking. These individual variations add to the richness of the course, but they must also be tempered by concern for consistency in the evaluation of students. It takes a lot of give and take to reach agreement on what each of us will require of students.

There are virtually no problems with administrators, but staffing is a continuing problem, since the normal work load for teaching assistants in the history department is much lighter than that required by "The American Experience." In the orthodox history courses, teaching assistants are little more than glorified graders. Here, they must lead three discussion sections, each with twenty-two students, attend lectures, and grade tests and assignments.

Nevertheless, all of these problems seem trivial in comparison to the main obstacle that we have encountered in teaching critical thinking—the effect on students of twelve years of elementary and secondary schooling. When it is compared to other nations, the United States is clearly one of the leading democracies in the world. The oratory of the Fourth of July rings true. But we recognize that the process of socialization, and particularly the process of political socialization, falls far short of those democratic ideals. Most of those who socialize our children are concerned not with the Jeffersonian model of the democratic citizen but with maintaining a familiar system. They regard each new generation as a band of barbarians unless and until its members are indoctrinated in certain basic values and learn to accept the system as it is—indeed, to be proud of the system and to defend it without question. All of the major agents of socialization—the family, the schools and churches, and the media—contribute to this process, but the schools, I believe, have the biggest impact, which is problematic for those who would teach critical thinking.

Texas is more conservative than much of the country, and the problem for us is more acute. A survey of the Houston Independent School District in 1969 and 1970 revealed that, of the 198 school teachers who responded, only eleven (5.6 percent) were completely willing to allow discussion of controversial political or social questions in the classroom. Virtually all reacted negatively to the idea of greater freedom for students, and the majority were conservative on race and economic issues as well (Kraemer and Newell, 1979, p. 23). These findings bear out Ehman's (1970, p. 78) assertion that "Teachers are most interested in teaching the status quo and transmitting values than rationally analyzing controversy and values of the society."

The result is that most students are quite unprepared for our course. They have not been taught to participate in their own education. They are passive, reactive, noninitiating recipients of "knowledge." For many of our students, education consists of having someone show them knowledge, comprehension, and application—the categories at the lower end of Bloom's taxonomy. They have been deprived of discussion of controversial topics. They have been taught to accept the system, not to question it. They have been "educated for docility," as Charles Silberman (1970) once put it.

Our task, as we see it, is to convince these students that they can and should participate in their own education, that controversy is real and important, that facts do not constitute knowledge, that being critical and discussing unpleasant and difficult aspects of society are not forms of disloyalty, and that they can and should form opinions of their own on difficult questions and be able to support and defend them. Instead of indoctrinating students with attitudes and values and then having them learn facts to support these attitudes and values (the procedure used in the public schools), we try to reverse this process by having students discover and examine the facts first and then draw conclusions about attitudes and values. This is not easy.

Our success has been mixed. We hardly touch some students. They seal us out and get through the course as they got through public school, without commitment and by repeating enough of what they had read and heard to pass. A few students actively reject us and the course, or they regard the course as merely another form of objectionable indoctrination. A small minority of our students views us as radicals. However, many respond positively, and a few even tell us that we have transformed their lives. Since many of these comments are made after the course is over and grades assigned, we tend to believe them.

It would be unreasonable to expect an about-face in students' classroom behavior merely as the result of one course, although some students have told us that we had a profound influence. I hope that my colleagues will put less emphasis on facts and more on critical thinking in their students—selfishly, we would like what we have taught to be reinforced. This emphasis makes teaching more challenging and sometimes more difficult, but I have found it unequivocally rewarding for both student and teacher.

My participation in this course has been one of the joys of my teaching, because I think that we do influence many of our students. It can be infuriating when they sit quietly and take dutiful notes on some particularly provocative thing one or another of us has said. I want to shake them and say, "Don't just write that down. Tell me what you think of it." In fact, I have said things like that in class, even though I know that it is difficult to speak up in a class of that size. It gratifies me to know that most students eventually will speak up in their discussion sections. I said earlier that teaching the course had allowed us to discover new facets of ourselves, our students, and our disciplines. I think that the course has helped to teach me humility. I think I am less formal with students, more willing to accept them as they are, more tolerant of their imperfections, and at the same time more ambitious for them in my educational goals. We enjoy the course, so we enjoy each other. With regard to my discipline, I am much less concerned with trying to make political scientists out of my students and much more concerned with helping them to find things in politics and government that will help them in their development as thinking people and ultimately as human beings. Perhaps I ascribe too much to the course, but these are the kinds of changes that have taken place in me during my ten years of planning and teaching "The American Experience."

The Students' View

Just as instructors experience highs and lows in teaching critical thinking, students encounter rewards and problems in learning it. We asked students how they felt about being in a course where a heavy emphasis is placed on critical thinking. Almost without exception, their replies indicated that the challenge to their thinking was what had made the course a valuable experience for them. As one put it, "I liked the course, not necessarily because I agreed with everything [the instructors] said, but because I was stirred to think about things on which I had never really held an opinion." In the words of another student, "I always disliked history and government, because in high school it was boring and lacked any sort of challenge. This course was moving, but most importantly it challenged students to reflect on the material, to draw conclusions on their own—I liked that."

For these students and an overwhelming majority of their peers, the emphasis on critical thinking, on seeing new sides of old issues, on analyzing the logic behind beliefs that they had always taken at face value was the driving force of the course. For some students, the class periods went far beyond the ordinary experience. As one student said, "I let mysef 'get into' the class and be affected by it. My friends would tell me I was taking the class 'too seriously'—that it was just a class. I don't think that's true. I'd respond, 'No, it's not just a class—it's people.'" Students found themselves going to great lengths not to miss class then coming away from class exhausted. "Sometimes I agreed with the instructors," said one student; "other times they pretty well ticked me off. Either way they never failed to really make me think about what they had said."

If this course was such an exciting experience for students, the next logical question is why. What aspects of the course produced this positive reaction in students? There was more variation in their answers to this question, but the answers seemed to center on three points: critical thinking as a goal, the use of controversial material to foster critical thinking, and willingness of instructors to set an example and to take a position on each question.

Students recognized the critical thinking goal as an important one. As one expressed it, "For me it was particularly frustrating but valuable to have to listen to, think about, and talk over the ideas raised in the lectures. I really appreciated the fact that they expected us to make up our own minds and not just regurgitate facts like in so many other classes." Their responses indicated that students understood that they were learning a skill — the analysis of ideas — and an attitude — the willingness to question and probe rather than merely accept — both of which would serve them well in other courses and in their everyday lives.

Course content served also to focus students' attention. The selection of controversial issues for lectures and readings was designed to facilitate critical thinking, since many of the questions raised were new ideas for this fairly conservative student body. As noted earlier, the readings deal with topics like urban America, war and peace, and leadership. Rather than moving from the events which led to World War I to the events which led to World War II, the course focuses on the effects of war on the American character. Other topics, such as blue-collar workers, a segment of the population not usually studied in college courses, give students a perspective on how government policies affect individual lives. Rather than neutral facts, the course revolves around emotional issues, which touch the personal experiences of students and challenge their assumptions. Said one: "I found the lectures and the readings on war, especially Vietnam, enlightening. My dad fought there twice. Many of his friends were killed. I always thought that war was useless and horrible, but I never realized that the Vietnam war was so much more horrifying than the 'honorable' wars earlier in American history. I understand my father better because of those discussions."

The third aspect of the course most frequently mentioned by students is the personal involvement of the instructors themselves. Rather than standing apart from the information and presenting ideas as facts chiseled in stone, the instructors become very actively involved in their subject and take stands, which they are careful to identify as their own views. For example, one of the instructors had been a student radical during the 1960s. In discussing the protest movements of that decade, he used his own experiences to show how someone with his beliefs and attitudes would respond to the issues of the time. Many students felt that this personalization helped them to understand the ethos of the time. "Most of my life my instructors seemed to stress impartiality and aloofness. It's refreshing to find that others hold deep emotional convictions, too," said one student. "I admire the quality of the instructors who were willing to express their own opinions and speak out for what they believed," said another. "I have really liked having a personal viewpoint rather than facts straight from the book. It makes expressing my own opinions easier."

For many students, this tendency among the instructors to voice their own opinions, combined with their selection of controversial topics, struck home to their conservative belief structures and made them want to reply. This would have been far more difficult if the topics under discussion had been more straightforward or if the views had been presented as facts. Too many students have been trained to expect that instructors will only present facts—statements of truth not open to debate. Early schooling does not encourage the child to challenge the statements made by instructors, textbooks, newspapers, or television. If the student's experience runs counter to the stated fact, the student is taught to question his own interpretation rather than the "authority." When he learns, however, that not all "facts" are necessarily true, but subject to interpretation, he takes the first step on the path to becoming an independent, critical thinker. When an instructor presents ideas as interpretations tinged with his own biases, the student is more likely to take the first step in viewing those ideas with a critical eye. The instructor becomes less of an authority and more of an equal, which encourages the student to speak up for his own ideas.

Nevertheless, no bed of roses would be complete without thorns, and no course would be complete without problems. This course is no exception. Ironically, just as the joys of this course arise from its focus on critical thinking, so do its problems. Two problems that seem to trouble students, grading and content coverage, are probably found in any course where critical thinking is the focus.

It should come as no surprise that, when we asked students to describe their frustrations with the course, the area of testing and grading was mentioned first by many students. Grades were based on students' participation in discussion, critical essays on a variety of topics, and essay tests requiring critical analysis and evaluation. One typical test question has already been described. Other test questions have required students to describe their own political socialization and to evaluate that process by democratic principles and practices. Topics for critical essays come from experiences like a float trip on the Colorado River through the city of Austin; students are asked to describe in detail the nature and extent of municipal services provided to each neighborhood encountered along the way. Sometimes, they are asked to show their thinking in short story form. Last year, one student wrote a fine parody of *Plunkett of Tammany Hall,* set in Texas. Testing and grading emphasize how students discuss an issue rather than what they discuss. Many students, however, find it difficult to understand the criteria by which their responses are judged. As one frustrated student put it, "My TA tells us there are no right or wrong answers to the questions, but instead your grade is based on if he agrees with what you believe. This is no way to handle six hours of GPA. I realize it would be difficult to make a test pertaining to this course multiple choice or fill in the blank, and I can see the reason for having essay tests, but sometimes it is hard to find what the TA is looking for and that's not what this class is all about. A person may know the material well and never miss a lecture or discussion class and his grade may not reflect it."

This frustration with ambiguity has surfaced frequently. When students are asked to define critical thinking, they have no trouble producing definitions which parallel those of the instructors and teaching assistants. But when it comes to translating the definitions into behavior, they seem to founder. Confronted with test questions, essay assignments, and discussion topics for which there are no "correct" answers, they feel they have no way of knowing how their answers will be received.

Students also show concern about inconsistency between different discussion sections. The individuality of the teaching assistants and the students themselves means that each section is a unique experience, not easily compared to the rest. For students accustomed to uniformity and factual answers, the metaprocessing that is needed to evaluate critical thinking and its developmental progress is sometimes too subtle, particularly when a grade is on the line. Many have difficulty understanding how two diametrically opposed views can be arrived at by the same careful analytical process and how both can therefore represent correct answers in the eyes of an evaluator.

A second problem for students was the need to "cover" the content in preparation for future courses. In the opinion of one student, "This course needs to emphasize some of the basics covered in the two courses it is a substitute for better than it does. I am especially concerned that a lot of information I could have learned in Government 310 was lost by taking this course." Another student voiced the same concern in other terms: "I enjoyed the topic orientation of the course much more than I would have a chronology, but I worry that I won't be ready for other courses. I've learned a lot, but what will happen when I hit a more standard 'tell me the facts' course?"

Although students were articulate about the meaning of critical thinking and appreciative of a class which challenged their thinking, they seemed to be uncomfortable with a course in history and government which had an abstraction for its primary focus. Perhaps the virtues of a liberal education have been lost on this generation of students. Their past schooling may have reinforced the concrete, by often avoiding the abstract. When students are placed in a situation which asks for analysis, synthesis, and evaluation, they feel unsure, since their finely honed skills of memorization are no longer enough. Students need the opportunity to learn that the mechanisms of thought survive the test of time, while the facts change with each new discovery.

Problems of grading and content aside, the greatest difficulty for students in this course has proved to be dissonance that arises from controversial issues and from the positions that instructors take on those issues. Said one student: "The class was always interesting and informative, but I do think the views presented were all one-sided. Most of the thoughts thrown out to us were left-wing. I think the class might have benefited more if we had been presented with two viewpoints on such relevant topics as arms control, type of government the U.S. has, and rights of citizens as citizens." Students admire the fact that their instructors voice opinions and choose issues that are arguable, current, and close to the students' experience. Nevertheless, the clash of views is inevitable. The instructors often present their opinions vividly and emotionally, hoping to encourage the students to think carefully. While students admit that such tactics caused them to evaluate their own attitudes, they found it uncomfortable to hear some ideas. At first glance, this effect may appear to be negative. But if one probes students more deeply, one may find that a lot of critical thinking has been taking place.

"I felt they played with our emotions a lot but maybe that was their way of having us think about topics," said one student. "I believed at first that both of the instructors were too opinionated, and it bothered me that they only expressed one viewpoint a lot of times in class," said another. "But, because it angered me at times, I began to go out on my own to find the answer—the one that would satisfy myself." As a third student expressed it, "I feel they've taught me a different lesson—to question everyone and everything, to see as objectively as possible both sides of the coin and to decide within myself what is the truth." These thoughts (rather "critical" ones, we believe), when taken together with the others quoted here, speak of the joys and frustrations that students feel in the face of the unknown. In a course in which the content and method are not what they have come to expect, they do not know how to evaluate their own progress except by saying that they certainly are enjoying themselves. For many students, this in itself is a new experience. It is reasonable for them to have such mixed feelings, as we all know from our own experience. Students know that they are participating in something important, but they have not learned the skills required for coping with the things being asked of them.

Finally, the most important aspect of a course is its ability to accomplish its goal. The goal of this course is to encourage critical thinking. Do students feel that they learn to think more critically? We have already seen that many students do believe that the course has its intended effect. Very few students with whom we talked were unaffected by the course, and the response of most is typified in the words of one: "My ability to think critically is much better now than it used to be. Now I can take important issues and decide what my stand on the issue is, and I can also tell you exactly why." Almost without exception, the instructors and teaching assistants agree.

The Teaching Assistants' View

The teaching assistants are situated right in the middle of all the promise and prospect excited by this course. They are responsible for those activities where most critical thinking development occurs, the discussion sections, the critical essays, and tests. They are teachers of critical thinking, in every sense of that word. We asked the same questions of teaching assistants that we had asked of students and of the instructor, and we got some interesting insights into the course and the teaching of critical thinking.

Two of the teaching assistants were new to this assignment, while most had assisted in the course before. Most of those questioned said that assisting in this course had been different—and difficult. Said one: "I've assisted in a standard Government 310 course before, and it had a very traditional and factual perspective. Critical thinking was not a stated goal in those courses. I think we get away with it in here because it's an interdisciplinary course and the people who are doing it want to do it." Said another: "I think the students in this course are different from the regular Government 310 students. These students tend to be more flexible, more imaginative, more willing to gamble, maybe because this is a six-hour course." As a third put it, "We don't inform so much as we allow them to focus their opinion. In other courses, the goal is to inform, and they become boring. The most important thing here is the feeling of excitement." And in the words of a fourth, "Being a TA in 'The American Experience' is a mixed blessing. We have a lot of say in what happens, but we also have a lot of responsibility. When a group is going well, it's fantastic. But when a group is bad, it's the worst."

The problems voiced by teaching assistants echoed those mentioned both by students and by the instructor. The teaching assistants all felt frustrated in their attempts to communicate to students what was expected of them in the critical essays that they were to write. Said one: "I think many of the students equate critical thinking with criticism, at least in the beginning. Or worse, they accept a different viewpoint just because it's different and think that's what I want in a critical essay."

On the microscale of the critical essay, the assistants experienced the problems of teaching critical thinking that all instructors face on the macroscale of liberal education. We seem to be able to agree on general principles, but when grading is the issue, we cannot communicate the specifics. Our teaching assistants have not reported any way of dealing with this problem that has proved overwhelmingly effective.

Some have attempted to introduce their students to Bloom's taxonomy, showing them how each level produces a different perspective in the handling of the course material. Some try to model the type of analysis they wish to communicate by direct participation in class discussions and individual conferences on topic essays. Their most effective tool is extensive feedback on each essay, which emphasizes the analytical aspect while deemphasizing the details.

The same stumbling block—the communication of expectations—confronts the assistants when they try to evaluate the discussion sections. As one assistant put it, "I really feel uncomfortable having to assign a grade to the discussion participation, even though I know how important it is. I think it's necessary to get them talking and to establish an open, egalitarian atmosphere. But if I have to keep taking notes about who said things, that sure stifles spontaneity, both for them and for me. So I'm reduced to trying to form impressions of what's going on, and I know that's unfair. A lot of students are quiet in class, but when they make a comment, it's obvious that they're really thinking about the issues." The assistants have no firm answers to offer on ways of resolving the problem. They use questions to draw out those who are quiet or ask them to voice the ideas that they have presented in their essays. All the assistants try to emphasize the idea of equality in participation by minimizing their own role as group leader. No one was able to suggest an ultimately objective way of accurately grading students' work in discussion sections, but all felt that its benefits outweighed the difficulties.

Assistants also reflected the students' concern for the idea of "covering" the material. As one teaching assisant said, "I have a lot of trouble reconciling my own need to get a good balance of discussion on readings and lecture material with the students' need to explore questions they see in the topics. If they're really into a topic and doing a lot of good thinking, it's like tossing cold water on them to try to bring the discussion back to the topic. I haven't yet learned how to do that gracefully, or even decided if I should do it." Said another: "I have questions about whether we provide them with a cognitive basis or whether we are just manipulating their emotions."

Teaching assistants felt that the content issue was especially strong in discussion sections, when students were looking to them for "correct" answers. According to one assistant, "The students keep trying to back me up to the wall to find out what I really think, as if that were the truth. I think they have great difficulty disagreeing with the instructor, because of the grading issue and because of their view of the instructor as an authority."

Despite their belief in the goals of this course, the teaching assistants were placed in a difficult position by these problem areas. The teaching assistants want the course to succeed, but they are painfully aware of the practical problems that they are facing. One summarized it this way: "The main impression I can remember having the first semester I assisted in this course was that this was really different. Every class was exciting. This semester has really been hard. It just doesn't feel the same. My feeling about this course is that every discussion group should be good. This semester I can't get it going, and we're all suffering because of it."

An Administrator's View

Finally, we quizzed administrators about this course that tries to foster critical thinking. As already mentioned, the course originated in the desire of one dean to encourage interdisciplinary study. Administratively, the course was originally housed in the Division of General and Comparative Studies. That division had nourished interdisciplinary thinking, and it was a place where things could happen that could not happen otherwise. The psychological effect of housing the course in that division was to encourage all those involved to move away from their stereotypes of history and government courses toward a more general educational goal of metaskills, such as critical thinking.

This administrative structure brought problems of its own. Because the division did not have a faculty of its own but had to borrow faculty from departments in other administrative units, there were constant problems of budgeting, credit hour assignments, and responsibility. The division has since been absorbed into the College of Liberal Arts under a single administrator. This should ease some of the administrative problems that courses such as "The American Experience" have encountered. The dean of the college described the problems and our solution in very pragmatic terms: "Before, we were constantly running into problems with bureaucracy. Departments were often unwilling to lend their faculty to such endeavors. I believe that interdisciplinary studies will be much facilitated by the single administrative unit. Now I can encourage department X to lend faculty in return for other considerations they might be seeking from me." Apparently, the interdisciplinary nature of "The American Experience," which is an important aspect of its critical thinking goal, has the support of those whose decisions can make or break a course. That is important for several reasons. Department chairpersons take their cues for support or nonsupport of people and programs from the dean. Also, the dean actively controls the number of teaching assistants available for each course and sometimes the assignments as well. Without the active support of the dean, the course might have withered away. A course of this nature often demands more in time and resources than traditional courses, and those involved—faculty, teaching assistants, and students—need reinforcement and real support from the administrative system of the institution.

Aside from supporting flexible administrative structures and doing a little horsetrading for faculty time, the administrators we talked to seemed to prefer to stay out of the way. As one of them said, "I usually don't get involved in a course unless someone starts to complain, and no one has been complaining about 'The American Experience' yet."

Conclusions

"The American Experience" is a fascinating course. It has many strikes against it: it is required, it is large, and its content—history and government—not only are old hat to most students but considered boring by many as well. Worst of all, the instructors are trying to teach a complex skill that is usually reserved for small, upper-division seminars. In spite of it all, however, students and instructors continue to be excited by the class. Why is this so? After analyzing all the interviews and assessments obtained from participants, we believe that the effort to focus the course on critical thinking makes the difference. This is not to say that the course is always successful or that everyone involved is always happy. Quite the contrary. Frustration is evident in all parties, but it is not the frustration which comes from the pursuit of useless goals. We feel that the joys and concerns expressed by participants in this one course are probably echoed by the many others who are grappling with the difficulties of making the goal of critical thinking a practical reality. We think that our experience with "The American Experience" offers encouragement to them.

References

Bloom, B. S. (Ed.). *Taxonomy of Educational Objectives. Handbook I: Cognitive Domain.* New York: McKay, 1956.

Ehman, L. H. "Normative Discourse and Attitude Change in the Social Studies Classroom." *The High School Journal,* 1970, *54,* 78.

Howell, J. T. *Hard Living on Clay Street.* New York: Doubleday, 1973.

Kraemer, R. H., and Newell, C. *Texas Politics.* St. Paul, Minn.: West, 1979.

Krathwohl, D. R., and others. *Taxonomy of Educational Objectives: Handbook II: Affective Domain.* New York: McKay, 1964.

Niehardt, J. C. *Black Elk Speaks.* Lincoln: University of Nebraska Press, 1979.

Silberman, C. E. *Crisis in the Classroom: The Remaking of American Education.* New York: Random House, 1970.

Smith, L. E. *Killers of the Dream.* New York: Harper & Row, 1969.

Wright, R. *Native Son.* New York: Harper & Row, 1969.

Marilla D. Svinicki received her Ph.D. degree in experimental psychology from the University of Colorado and is currently assistant director of the Center for Teaching Effectiveness at the University of Texas at Austin.

Richard H. Kraemer, the author of several books on national and Texas politics, received his Ph.D. degree from the University of Texas and is currently an associate professor of government at the University of Texas at Austin.

Assessing success in critical thinking—the most complicated kind of learning—presents difficulties to both teachers and students. Yet testing may be the most effective way of fostering critical thinking.

Testing for Critical Thinking: Issues and Resources

Robert E. Young

Teachers in American colleges and universities give students tests in enormous numbers. Milton and Edgerly (1977) estimate that about ten million tests are given each year. Undoubtedly, some of these tests attempt to measure critical thinking, the kinds of skills and activities to which this volume has addressed itself. The question is, "How well do we do it?"

Teachers and students often share the perception of a teacher of history on my campus: "In spite of all the classwork in building hypotheses, solving problems, and critical thinking, when it comes to test time we are back to rote." If learning of this kind is more difficult to foster, it may also be harder to measure. Milton and Edgerly (1977) found that the learning tested by most of the tests they examined was far less complex than the learning required for critical thinking. They also found widespread dissatisfaction with testing and grading in general. It stands to reason that measures of the most complicated of learning may present difficulties to both teachers and students. This chapter will try to shed some light on the issues involved in measuring critical thinking and identify resources to assist teachers and colleges.

Many good and useful volumes have been written on the measurement of student performance (for example, Anderson and others, 1975; Dressel and Associates, 1961; Ebel, 1972; Grondlund, 1976; Heywood, 1977; Lenning, 1977; Thorndike, 1971). There are also a number of useful guides for classroom teachers (Bloom, Hastings, and Madaus, 1971; Green, 1975; Grondlund, 1973; Grondlund, 1977; Mager, 1973; Payne, 1974). Even specific subject areas have been covered: science (Nedelsky, 1965; Nelson, 1967), math (Berg, 1965; Merwin and Higgins, 1968), music (Colwell, 1970), and foreign languages (Lado, 1964).

In almost every case, these works develop the same line of thinking about testing. "Classroom evaluation is viewed as an integral part of the teaching-learning process. It involves three fundamental steps: (1) identifying and defining the intended learning outcomes, (2) constructing or selecting tests or other evaluation instruments that are relevant to the specified outcomes, and (3) using the results to improve learning and instruction" (Grondlund, 1976, pp. vii–viii). The references listed above deal among them with each step in detail. They give advice and examples for each phase of testing. For that reason they are important resources for classroom teachers. Here, I want to consider each step as it relates to the testing of critical thinking.

Outcomes

In their chapters for this volume, the authors have attempted to identify and define the outcomes of instruction for critical thinking. The authors have tried to describe how they have come to describe critical thinking or a special aspect of it, such as problem solving. As their chapters suggest, they have looked to a variety of sources.

In the introductory essay, we cited a definition of critical thinking and a set of outcomes proposed in an early study of general education (Dressel and Mayhew, 1954, pp. 177–180): "the ability to define a problem, the ability to select pertinent information for the solution of the problem, the ability to recognize stated and unstated assumptions, the ability to formulate and select relevant and promising hypotheses, and the ability to draw conclusions validly and to judge the validity of inferences."

Two issues are important concerning outcomes, particularly for the testing of critical thinking: Where do they come from? How can they be defined for the purposes of writing test questions?

Sources of Objectives for Critical Thinking. Each teacher will have to identify the specific critical thinking skills and abilities that he or she wishes to teach and test. This can be done idiosyncratically, if the teacher uses his or her own conceptions to define what critical thought means for his or her discipline. As an alternative, the teacher can begin with existing definitions to stimulate his or her own thinking or to identify objectives directly.

One extremely useful source has been the taxonomy of educational objectives developed by Bloom and others (1956). Concerned as they were about examining college students, those involved in this project attempted to classify those student behaviors which they thought represented the intended outcomes of the educational process. In the cognitive domain, they defined and ordered those behaviors from the simplest (knowledge) to the most complex (comprehension, application, analysis, synthesis, and evaluation, in that order). Regardless of the concept of critical thinking that a teacher adopts, each of these abilities will have an important place in the instruction supplied by that teacher. These abilities would need to be taught and tested. Bloom (1956, p. 186) proposes that the most complex ability, evaluation, involves some combination of the simpler skills. In this scheme, evaluation is the making of judgments about the value of ideas, works, solutions, methods, and materials, in terms of internal or external criteria. As a teacher, I might want to assist the development of this judgment ability in my course, or I might want to focus on its component skills—application, analysis, or synthesis, which are valuable in themselves—and leave evaluation itself to another time and place.

National commissions, professional associations, state and local groups, and individual scholars and teachers continue to propose outcomes for higher education, but the work of the Cooperative Study of Evaluation in General Education still remains the most extensive statement of objectives for critical thinking in higher education (Dressel and Mayhew, 1954). Task groups of college teachers from across the country developed and described objectives for the teaching and testing of critical skills in the major curricular areas—social and natural sciences, humanities, and communication—in addition to the general outcomes listed above.

The character of the given discipline is an important source of objectives. Instruction for critical thinking most often takes place in the framework of study of a specific subject. In an excellent chapter on "finding objectives," Heywood (1977, p. 165) takes Bloom's taxonomy to task for failure to "come to grips with subjects on their own terms." The teacher's intellectual and emotional commitment, he suggests, is to the terminology and literature of the discipline, its special "language" or manner of thinking. Using a delightful passage from Bloch's *The Historian's Craft,* Heywood (p. 165) observes: "Analysis of the writings of historians on the methods and problems of history reveals behavioral objectives and methods within the language used by historians about history and thus the emotional framework of its teachers. Moreover, they convey the excitement and motivation of the authors in their own work."

My own discipline, psychology, has seen a continuing debate over competing explanations of human behavior. Psychologists have labels—for example, behaviorist, cognitivist, humanist—which have both general and specific meanings. As one outcome of my courses, I want students to be able to evaluate the contribution that each theory makes to their own understanding of behavior. To do this, they will need to consider the special commitments of the discipline as well as their own.

Defining Objectives for Testing. Each of these sources—existing definitions and taxonomies, the nature of disciplines, and personal conceptions—will suggest critical thinking outcomes of a general form. But to test and measure a student's ability, a more specific form needs to be developed for the objectives of our teaching. This is where the general skills of critical thinking, such as "the ability to define a problem," are matched to the content of our courses. For example, a teacher of economics or business might want students to be able to "define the problems which inflation creates for a small business." With testing in mind, we need to begin to define those things that will evidence critical thinking in the particular course.

To return to my own example, if I have used Bloom's taxonomy as a source of outcomes and decided as a result to foster evaluation, I have to decide exactly what I want my students to learn to evaluate. In a course on the history of higher education, I may want students to be able to evaluate each major item of federal legislation that we study for its impact on undergraduate and graduate curricula. My job then is to decide what instances of knowledge, comprehension, application, analysis, and synthesis are required to do this kind of critical thinking. These become the objectives that I will teach and also test.

In defining outcomes, we are identifying not only content but also what students will do with it. We are not describing learning experiences or what we intend to do during instruction; we are describing the results of students' experiences and instruction. The focus is on the student and on the actions of which the student is or is not capable. Whether the student can think critically must be inferred from these actions.

This specification assists both students and teachers. The more precisely students know what to expect, the more effectively they can prepare themselves and the more forcefully they can respond to our questions. In the realm of critical thinking, as in other areas, students often find themselves subjected to what Battersby (1973, p. ix) describes as an "instability of criteria—which contributes substantially to the production of safe, timid, non-grade-point-average-threatening work." If students do not know what counts for critical thinking, they will parrot our analyses or string facts together, hoping that thoroughness will substitute for incisiveness.

A clear idea of outcomes tells teachers which specific skills students must be helped to learn and practice. Defining objectives also helps us to communicate assignments and exam questions to students clearly.

A number of references are helpful when general outcomes must be defined for testing purposes. Grondlund (1973), Heywood (1977), Mager (1973), and Metfessel and Michael (1967) are especially helpful. Bloom, Hastings, and Madaus (1971) take the general statements of intellectual skills and abilities from Bloom's taxonomy to illustrate objectives and test questions for a number of specific subject areas.

Test Construction

With outcomes in mind, it is time to find a way of testing for them. Assessing students' achievement in critical thinking means selecting an existing measure or developing a measure from scratch. Whether made or borrowed, measures can include not only the typical classroom tests but papers, projects, exercises, and even self-assessment. For convenience, we will refer to all these measures as "tests," but whether it is typical or innovative, a measure of critical thinking will present students with a question or problem requiring their use of the skills defined by the objectives of instruction.

Existing Tests of Critical Thinking. Two types of existing tests are typically available: those which you or your colleagues have used in the past, and published tests, which usually were produced by researchers, testing specialists, or groups of educators.

Most classroom tests in higher education are discarded after use. If the intent is to keep courses current in content and to make tests secure until test time, this practice makes sense. But with the testing of critical thinking in mind, this practice may eliminate an important testing resource. We expect many critical skills to be exhibited in a number of our courses. Though the content may differ from course to course and from level to level, questions used in the past can provide useful "forms" for new questions. Tests prepared by colleagues can expand this resource. Like other teaching skills, testing ability increases with experience. Past questions that have proved themselves effective in measuring student achievement may be used again to teach us about effective testing in the area. Also, it takes less time to revise old test items than it does to create new ones. One study found that it takes five times less time, and that the revised items were more strongly related to course achievment (Lange, Lehman, and Mehrens, 1967).

To make old tests a resource simply requires that we keep them at ready access, together with some indication of the objectives they were intended to measure and of how well they worked. The latter could include statistical analyses of difficulty and discrimination, descriptions of students' reactions during the testing period and after, and your own assessment of how well each item measured what you intended to measure. Groups of teachers and departments and colleges could keep files of tests and analyses. This kind of resource could prove to be especially useful to new instructors.

Over the past thirty years, there have been some worthy attempts to define critical thinking and to design tests and procedures that can measure it. The published literature provides a small yet useful number of procedures, instruments, and items for testing critical thinking skills. Much of this work was done with research or the evaluation of educational programs as its purpose. Yet classroom teachers can benefit from taking a look at these materials. Some can be used as is to measure students' performance in our courses. Others provide models or ideas for ways of assessing particular thinking skills.

The test most frequently used in research and evaluation is the Watson-Glaser Critical Thinking Appraisal (Watson and Glaser, 1964). Based on Dressel and Mayhew's (1954) definition of critical thinking, it includes five subtests in two parallel forms to measure inference, recognition, deduction, interpretation, and evaluation of arguments. McCollum and Rosen (1972) developed exercises around controversial and neutral topics which try to tap the same thinking dimensions. The Experience of College Questionnaire developed by McDowell and Chickering (1967) takes another approach. Using Bloom's taxonomy, this instrument assesses behaviors associated with critical thinking in self-reports from students. Knopp and Stoker (1966) and Warren (1978) have developed other Bloom-based tests of students' competence. Two tests described by Winter (1979) may be of special note: Test of Thematic Analysis tests students' ability to form complex concepts and Analysis of Argument is a measure of intellectual flexibility—the ability to perceive all sides of a complicated and controversial issue. Though it is not limited to instruction in higher education, the collection of items described by Morse and McClure (1977) has been frequently used. Finally, Dressel and Mayhew (1954) is still a good source of items and procedures for testing critical thinking, especially in the four major discipline areas.

Teacher-Made Tests. Published tests usually provide a reliable and consistent measure of achievement, but if they test skills that are not those being taught, they lose their validity as measures of student ability. For an exam to be valid and fair (students' chief concern), it must measure achievement as defined and as taught. In other words, tests used to measure critical thinking must be consistent with the objectives for critical thinking. The published tests listed above will vary in the definitions that they give to critical thinking and in the particular aspects of critical thinking on which they focus.

If there is no previous or published test that measures critical thinking as you have defined and taught it, or if the use of a previous or published test seems inappropriate, then you will have to construct a new test of your own to measure students' achievement of your goals for critical thinking. The great majority of tests are teacher-made, and though some teachers may find existing tests useful, the likelihood is that college teachers will continue to determine how critical thinking will be assessed. Again, there are useful resources (listed above) to assist teachers with test construction. Dressel and associates (1961) describe approaches that may be used in natural science, social science, humanities, and communication skills. Karris (1978) will be useful for history, Poppenfus and Paradise (1978) for social science, and Doran (1978) for science.

Books about testing are full of good principles. As a rule, reliability and validity usually get the most attention. These books also suggest useful methods and procedures. As noted above, a paper and pencil test is not the only or even the most appropriate way of assessing critical thinking. Lenning (1978) presents a laundry list of methods, which ranges from anecdotal records to troubleshooting exercises. Knapp and Sharon (1975) describe a number of "action" methods, including work samples, unobtrusive measures, and simulations. Glaser and Damrin (1954) have developed a performance test format for problem solving called the Tab Item, which has been used in vocational and medical education and which has promise for other areas.

All these methods have one thing in common. They involve the asking of questions or the posing of problems. The skill required on the part of the teacher in asking questions and posing problems may be the most critical factor involved in the teaching and testing of critical thinking. In a book delightfully titled *The Art of Interrogation,* Hamilton (1929, p. 86) proposes that "examining, . . . broadly conceived, is the art of assessing minds by means of questions." Considerable work has been done on questioning, but most of it has been applied to classroom activities; the application of this work to testing for critical thinking may provide yet another resource to teachers.

Questioning. Earlier in the chapter, I described the *Taxonomy of Educational Objectives* as a source of objectives for critical thinking. Norris Sanders has written a book titled *Classroom Questions: What Kinds?* (1966), in which he uses Bloom's (1956) scheme. Sanders suggests ways of developing questions for all levels in the taxonomy, and his principal aim is to influence classroom activities. Nevertheless, his book is useful in developing questions to foster thinking (application, analysis, synthesis, and evaluation) both for classroom use and for testing.

The kind of question that is asked influences the kind of thinking that is used to prepare a reply. Questions that ask "why" or "how," as compared to questions that ask "what," "where," and "when," are usually thought to require the kind of mental activity we have called critical thinking. This is not always true. Questions to which students bring an unusual knowledge of the subject matter or which have already been answered in class may require only memory for an answer. For example, if students are asked to assess the effects of industrial waste on the ecosystem of lower Lake Michigan, some may respond with a pat answer from yesterday's *Chicago Tribune,* or they may feel directed by the question to demonstrate their thinking about a particular type of waste or a particular type of plant or wildlife. That's why Sanders' (1966) scheme is useful in analyzing our questions and in stimulating the development of test questions, problems, and projects that truly require critical thought.

Sanders describes how to develop questions on each level of the taxonomy, and he gives examples. Let me briefly use the example I have been developing in this chapter. Recall that I have chosen to emphasize evaluation, and have developed specific objectives around the effects of legislation on college and university curricula. Now it is time to develop test questions and procedures. To give some variety to my own reading and to force students to develop their own resources, I could ask them to do a case study of one specific curriculum. The questions I would ask are these: What criteria would you use to judge the effects of legislation on a curriculum? Use these criteria to evaluate each piece of legislation. Rank order this legislation for its impact on your curriculum. Which pieces of legislation favored the curriculum? Which did it harm?

It is useful to use the following sequence when planning and preparing questions: Choose a topic from a course and write a question from each level of the taxonomy. (This can be a good way of specifying objectives.) Then ask yourself what types of answers you would expect for each question and level. Compare your questions and expected answers with the descriptions and examples in Bloom (1956) or Sanders (1966). Ask a colleague to react to your questions. Finally, use these questions, and observe whether they lead to the kinds of thinking that you intended. This sequence can help to ensure that test questions follow from course objectives, which is the only guarantee of a valid test of students' abilities.

We want our tests to be consistent not only with course objectives but also with what we do in class. Do we ask the same kinds of questions in class that we ask on tests? Often we do not! Sometimes, we raise and answer thinking questions in our lectures, discussions, and exercises, yet on exams our questions require only memory. At other times, we do just the opposite. One procedure can be helpful to check up on our consistency: audiotape a typical class session, review the tape and note the questions asked, identify the level of thinking that each question required; do the same for several old exams, and compare the results.

In addition to Bloom (1956) and Sanders (1966), there are a number of useful works on crafting questions to stimulate and assess student thinking (Dauterman, 1970; Fraenkel, 1960; Hunkins, 1976; Morgan and Schrieber, 1969; Tinsley, 1973). Winne (1979) reviews research on the relationship between questions intended to stimulate application, analysis, synthesis, and evaluation and students' achievement.

Using Results to Improve Learning and Teaching

Tests and the kinds of questions that we ask can influence critical thinking. Also, the results of these tests—the answers to questions and the solutions to problems posed on these tests—can be used with students to further strengthen the skills that we hope to foster. Most exams are constructed to allow efficient determination of the number of correct answers and to provide data for award of a grade. They are often seen in isolation, as ends in themselves, and little attention is given to the way in which students have formed their answers or to the relation of performance on one exam to performance on the next. If teachers gave some attention to process and development, then tests could become a means of fostering critical thinking.

In a short book appropriately titled *Typical Folly: Evaluating Student Performance in Higher Education,* James L. Battersby (1973, p. 37) cites an example not unfamiliar to college teachers working in any subject area:

> I once asked a young girl who had recently been working with multiplication tables if she could multiply twenty-five by twenty-five. She had not before encountered a problem quite as complex as this, but after pausing a minute to consider and calculate, she came up with sixty-five. The "correct" answer, of course, was 625, and I could not understand how she had arrived at such a grossly inaccurate figure. When I asked her how much twenty-five plus twenty-five was, she immediately said fifty, without realizing that that figure was only slightly less than her total for twenty-five times twenty-five. Now, if I were simply interested in whether she could answer my question "correctly" or not, I would have discovered nothing about the ingenuity of her mind. The fact is that her answer is perfectly sensible, and her result is absolutely "correct"; as long as the figures are construed as they were by the young girl, the answer will be sixty-five. Her reasoning: five times five is twenty-five; write the five

> below the line and carry the two; now add the three two's in the left-hand column to get six and, hence, a total of sixty-five. Confronted with a totally new mathematical situation (well, almost totally new), the child rapidly conceived a working hypothesis that would yield a confirmable result; this, I submit, is sophisticated problem solving, but I would have discovered nothing about her genius if I had not paid attention to what she was doing.

If we are to determine with some certainty whether a student knows how to use information to solve particular problems, we need to have some idea of how the student goes about solving the problem, in addition to the solution produced. Battersby (p. 25) adds:

> . . . it is clear that some wrong answers are less significant than others: an error must be traced to its sources before it can be properly evaluated. Answers are wrong for different reasons, and errors are differently sophisticated.
>
> What the instructor most wants to know, I think, is how well a student is able to think as a mathematician, historian, or whatever, and whether he can generate and resolve respectable intellectual problems. Among other things, he should know whether the error was careless (some point in a complex math computation), whether it was due to a temporary loss of memory (a fact or formula could have been applied if it were recalled; the intellectual operations could have been successfully performed if the exam, say, were open book), or whether the problem was beyond the intellectual power of the student (even with all the basic information supplied, he would have been unable to work it out).

When attention is paid to process, we have the necessary data for showing students where they err as well as for reinforcement of effective and even of creative thinking. Furthermore, if we ourselves are conscious of process, our students may learn to be reflective about how they think. In the introductory chapter to this volume, I described a professor who asked his students to discuss their experience of critical thinking in his course. Several students responded by describing and critiquing their approach to a particular problem or analysis. Students and teachers alike can benefit from direct instructions to students to describe the process of their approach to questions, problems, and assignments. Teachers of mathematics and science do just that with the statement "Show your work."

Student performance, such as critical thinking, should be evaluated over time. Battersby (1973, p. ix) again observes: "The most reliable information . . . is the pattern of achievement that a student makes manifest in the process of meeting specific academic problems over an extended period." Like the skills of effective communication, the skills of critical thinking take time to build. In college students, these skills are "developing," and at any point they are more or less refined. The assessment that is the most useful in this growth is that which reflects past achievement and sets the basis for future learning and assessment. As Battersby (p. ix) puts it, ". . . the grading assumption here is that only when the nature and quality of past performance is known in some detail can we begin to determine how the qualities of mind implicated in past effort may be expected to insinuate themselves in the future."

On my campus, teachers of composition collect students' papers as the semester proceeds, and they use them as benchmarks of students' progress. Each paper is examined in the light of the ones preceding. These composition teachers ask themselves and their students, "How does this thesis sentence compare to last week's? To last month's?" The errors in the paper under critique set the agenda for the next paper, and the accomplishments, if they are similar to those exhibited in past papers, justify the judgment that certain skills are well in place. Education in the arts has the same desirable feature. Critiques and portfolios allow teachers and students to take a look at the learning of complex skills and of the attitudes that accompany them over time, as a process of development rather than a finished product. I suggest that assessment of critical thinking can benefit from the same approach to foster the relevant skills and attitudes.

In this chapter, I have described a general approach to the testing of critical thinking and recommended specific resources which teachers and college staffs might use in constructing measures of critical thinking. Tests of thinking must meet the standards of fairness and accuracy required for any measure of student performance. As the goals for critical thinking take a more important place in curricula and courses and as the commitment to helping students develop critical abilities finds its place in our teaching, tests of thinking become more challenging, stimulating, and important for teachers and students alike.

References

Anderson, S., and others. *Encyclopedia of Educational Evaluation: Concepts and Techniques for Evaluating Education and Training Programs.* San Francisco: Jossey-Bass, 1975.

Battersby, J. L. *Typical Folly: Evaluating Student Performance in Higher Education.* Urbana, Ill.: National Council of Teachers of English, 1973.

Berg, H. D. (Ed.). *Evaluation in Social Studies.* 35th Yearbook. Washington, D.C.: National Council for the Social Studies, 1965.

Bloom, B. S. (Ed.). *Taxonomy of Educational Objectives. Handbook I: Cognitive Domain.* New York: McKay, 1956.

Bloom, B. S., Hastings, J. T., and Madaus, G. F. *Handbook on Formative and Summative Evaluation of Student Learning.* New York: McGraw-Hill, 1971.

Colwell, R. *Evaluation of Music Teaching and Learning.* Englewood Cliffs, N.J.: Prentice-Hall, 1970.

Dauterman, P. J. "Are There Any Questions?" *Alberta English 76,* Summer 1970, pp. 20-32.

Doran, R. L. "Measuring the Process of Science Objectives." *Science Education,* 1978, *62,* 19-30.

Dressel, P. L., and Associates. *Evaluation in Higher Education.* Boston: Houghton-Mifflin, 1961.

Dressel, P. L., and Mayhew, L. B. *General Education: Explorations in Evaluation.* Washington, D.C.: American Council on Education, 1954.

Ebel, R. L. *Essentials of Educational Measurement.* Englewood Cliffs, N.J.: Prentice-Hall, 1972.

Fraenkel, J. P. "Ask the Right Questions." *The Clearing House,* 1960, *41,* 199-203.

Glaser, R., and Damrin, D. E. "The Tab Item: A Technique for the Measurement of Proficiency in Diagnostic Problem Solving Tasks." *Educational and Psychological Measurement,* 1954, *14,* 283.

Grondlund, N. E. *Preparing Criterion-Referenced Tests for Classroom Instruction.* New York: Macmillan, 1973.

Grondlund, N. E. *Measurement and Evaluation in Teaching.* (3rd ed.) New York: Macmillan, 1976.

Grondlund, N. E. *Constructing Achievement Tests.* (2nd ed.) Englewood Cliffs, N.J.: Prentice-Hall, 1977.

Hamilton, E. R. *The Art of Interrogation.* New York: Harcourt, Brace, 1929.

Heywood, J. *Assessment in Higher Education.* London: Wiley, 1977.

Hunkins, F. P. *Involving Students in Questioning.* Boston: Allyn & Bacon, 1976.

Karris, R. W. "Writing Multiple Choice Questions: The Problem and Proposed Solution." *The History Teacher,* 1978, *11* (2), 211-218.

Knapp, J., and Sharon, A. *A Compendium of Assessment Techniques.* Princeton, N.J.: Educational Testing Service, 1975.

Knopp, R. P., and Stoker, H. W. *Construction and Validation of Tests of Cognitive Processes as Described in the Taxonomy of Educational Objectives.* Tallahassee, Fla.: U.S. Office of Education Cooperative Research Program, 1966.

Lado, R. *Language Testing: The Construction and Use of Foreign Language Tests.* New York: McGraw-Hill, 1964.

Lange, A., Lehman, I. J., and Mehrens, W. A. "Using Item Analysis to Improve Tests." *Journal of Educational Measurement,* 1967, *4,* 65-68.

Lenning, O. T. "Assessing Student Progress in Academic Achievement." In L. L. Baird (Ed.), *New Directions for Community Colleges: Assessing Student Academic and Social Progress,* no. 18. San Francisco: Jossey-Bass, 1977.

Lenning, O. T. "Assessing Student Educational Progress." *ERIC/Higher Education Research Currents.* Washington, D.C.: American Association for Higher Education, 1978.

McCollom, J. A., and Rosen, D. *Instructor's Manual: Development of Higher Level of Thinking Abilities.* Portland, Ore.: Northwest Regional Educational Laboratory, 1972.

McDowell, J., and Chickering, A. W. *Experience of College Questionnaires.* Plainfield, Vt.: Project on Student Development, 1967.

Mager, R. F. *Measuring Instructional Intent.* Belmont, Calif.: Fearon, 1973.

Merwin, J. C., and Higgins, M. J. "Assessing the Progress of Education in Mathematics." *Mathematics Teacher,* 1968, *61,* 130-135.

Metfessel, N. T., and Michael, W. C. "A Paradigm Involving Multiple Criterion Measures for the Evaluation of Effectiveness of School Programs." *Educational and Psychological Measurement,* 1967, *27,* 931.

Milton, O., and Edgerly, J. W. *The Testing and Grading of Students.* New Rochelle, N.Y.: *Change Magazine,* 1977.

Morgan, J. C., and Schrieber, J. E. *How to Ask Questions.* Washington, D.C.: National Council for Social Studies, 1969.

Morse, H. T., and McClure, G. H. *Selected Items for the Testing of Study Skills and Critical Thinking.* (5th ed.) Washington, D.C.: National Council for Social Studies, 1977.

Nedelsky, L. *Science Teaching and Testing.* New York: Harcourt Brace Jovanovich, 1965.

Nelson, C. H. *Testing and Evaluation in the Biological Sciences.* CUEBS Publication 20. Washington, D.C.: American Institute of Biological Sciences, 1967.

Payne, D. A. *The Assessment of Learning: Cognitive and Affective.* Lextingon, Mass.: Heath, 1974.

Poppenfus, J. R., and Paradise, L. V. "Social Studies Objectives in Theory and Practice." *Social Studies,* 1978, *69* (5), 200-203.

Sanders, N. *Classroom Questions: What Kinds?* New York: Harper & Row, 1966.

Thorndike, R. L. (Ed.). *Educational Measurement.* (2nd ed.) Washington, D.C.: American Council on Education, 1971.

Tinsley, D.C. "Use of Questions." *Educational Leadership,* May 1973, 710-713.

Warren, J. R. *The Measurement of Academic Competence.* Berkeley, Calif.: Educational Testing Service, 1978.

Watson, G., and Glaser, E. M. *Watson-Glaser Critical Thinking Appraisal Manual.* New York: Harcourt Brace Jovanovich, 1964.

Winne, P. H. "Experiments Relating to Teachers' Use of Higher Cognitive Questions to Student Achievement." *Review of Educational Research,* 1979, *49* (1), 13-50.

Winter, D. G. "Defining and Mcasuring the Competencies of a Liberal Education." *Current Issues in Higher Education,* No. 5. Washington, D.C.: American Association for Higher Education, 1979.

Robert E. Young, formerly associate director of the Center for Improving Teaching Effectiveness, is now director of the Office of Instructional Development at the University of North Dakota. He is interested in the thinking activities of both students and teachers in higher education. The incentive and idea for this book grew out of work with faculty members as they try to foster critical thinking among an increasingly diverse student body.

Courses and curricula devoted to critical thinking often do not go far enough. The skills and attitudes of practical reason and effective action should be taught as well.

The Next Agenda: Practical Reasoning and Action

Robert E. Young

Throughout this volume the authors have tried to identify sources and resources that teachers and college staffs can use to further their thinking about and instruction in critical thinking. We hope that this volume truly has been a "sourcebook" in that sense. While it is impossible to identify all the ideas and approaches being used to advance the teaching of critical thinking, we hope that we have added to knowledge, understanding, and interest in this area. A continuing education simply requires a regular review of the teaching-related journals, annual conference reports, and funded projects in higher education in general and in the specific disciplines; then experimentation with new methods (maybe some described in this volume) and reflection on our experience in trying to foster critical thinking.

In this final chapter, I want to pursue two themes that emerge from the separate chapters: the practical side of critical thinking and the relationship of critical thought to action. I think these themes give some direction to further thought and work in this area of curriculum and instructional development.

The teaching of critical thinking involves the development of a whole range of intellectual skills and attitudes. However, nothing ensures where or how these skills will be used or whether they will be used. James Kinney (this volume) has helped us see that students and faculty are aware of this fact; the curriculum does little to reinforce critical thought, and society seems to provide better pay for other skills. Kinney proposes that interest and success will increase only when intellectual skills are learned in real, meaningful contexts, rather than in the academic and artificial contexts in which most coursework takes place. Robert Yinger develops the same idea in his chapter. Most of the problems that we encounter daily are practical rather than theoretical, and the procedure required for solving them is initially uncertain. The question "Which method should I use to foster critical thinking?" is a practical one. The grounds and procedures for choosing a method have not been spelled out, at least for your particular course and the students whom you must teach, and once you do choose, you cannot predict the results with any certainty. This is like most of the issues we face each day.

Practical Reasoning

What to teach in higher education is the subject of a continuing debate. Recently, and important to a consideration of critical thinking, the controversy has centered on the kinds of intellectual and life skills that are most important and on the responsibility of higher education to foster them. The movement toward an increased vocational emphasis in the curriculum is well documented. Its rationale is well established, and that it has support is well known. But from the other side of the fence, we often hear charges like this (Schulz, 1980, p. 10): "The substitution of quanitative methods for abstract thought and analysis is transforming the haven of intellectuals into a laboratory for technicians."

There should be some middle ground between the promoters of purely vocational interests and the advocates of abstract thought and analysis. Colleges and universities today are neither a haven of intellectuals nor a training ground for technicians. Although postsecondary education is diverse, diffused, and even distempered at times, it has evolved a special role somewhere between the passionless inquiry of the ivory tower and the sometimes bland, sometimes electric realm of human affairs. Though colleges ranging from Harvard to Scott County Community value knowledge, careful analysis, and genius, they have taken on problems that beg certainty and purely procedural solutions: the environment, social justice, public health, economic progress, international cooperation. This middle ground is where practical reasoning could fit as an objective of higher education.

The Guided Design and ADAPT programs described by Stonewater are good examples. Both are problem-based, and, if you take a close look, the problems which put students in situations that matter to them are the ones that create the most excitement and real learning for students. Kraemer's course, "The American Experience," is both successful and congruent with the interest of students and society in higher education when it puts critical skills to the test of real questions and problems.

In these cases, thinking is a means, not an end. Barbara Biber (1977, p. 8) paraphrases John Dewey when she describes the end to which our means of teaching critical thinking should apply: ". . . the life of learning in childhood should be such as to create an acting, thinking man—not a scholastic type, clustered among dusty manuscripts in libraries. He has work to do in the world, to make it over—and so in childhood, in his formative years in school, he needs vital experiences through which to learn how to make a viable partnership of thinking and reasoning and doing and testing, and then thinking it all over again—until the end of time."

Our curriculum needs a focus in each discipline on practical problems, practical problems of the discipline as well as of the society. Students need and want not only to prepare themselves for occupation and citizenship but also to negotiate the life of the mind. How to learn about the physical world is every bit as practical a problem as how to save it. For each program and each course, we need to identify that "work to do in the world" for which our students must prepare. If we can do that, then helping them learn the skills required to do that work will make the teaching and learning of critical thinking much more than a bothersome necessity.

Action

Critical thinking encourages the student to act as a practitioner rather than as an observer. Yinger helps us to see that many of the approaches to critical thinking, even those described in this volume, have an important limitation. They stop with thought; they do not take students into action. Practical reasoning—the kind of outcome that that fulfills higher education's special place in modern society—implies action. Long ago, Aristotle distinguished theoretical reasoning—which pursues the question "What is the case?"—from practical thought, which tries to determine "What is to be done?" (Anscombe, 1957; Raz, 1978). In the realm of the practical, the processes of reasoning inevitably lead us to conclusions of the form "I ought to do such and such." Action is the next-to-last step of critical thinking. Only reflection on that action remains to complete the cycle.

Action is invoked in many curricula and some programs aimed at fostering problem solving and critical thinking. But most curricula and programs neither teach the skills and dispositions necessary for effective action nor encourage students to try out their understandings, analyses, and solutions in any real way. Recently, I had the opportunity to review a new general education curriculum. After careful debate, a faculty committee had recommended that instruction in written skills, mathematics, logic, and in aesthetics be strengthened. They offered this rationale: "The proposed curriculum aims to provide basic skills and knowledge for an understanding of and a functioning within the academic curriculum and the larger society in which students will live and work, and to lay a foundation for lifelong learning and thoughtful use of leisure time." Though action may be implied in the words, the effective character is cognitive and analytical. It is "preparation" for life, not life itself. If Kinney is right, students' education, including our intent to help them think critically, will be credible and successful only if we can meet them in the middle of the life that they know.

This idea has some problems. It strikes at the heart of the purposes of education and at the role of higher education. Also, to ask students to act on their reasoning presents difficulties both for them and for teachers. Below I suggest some approaches, but right now I propose that we need to *think* about the relationship between thinking and acting in our courses and curriculum.

Approaches to Practical Reasoning and Action

How do we create courses and curricula which help students learn to solve practical problems and act on their thinking? First, a kind of planning which puts the focus on practical, not theoretical, problems will be required. Joseph Schwab (1970) directs us to look for those problems with our students and other members of the society in the concrete situations that we face where we live and work. Only then will we know what our disciplines can contribute through curriculum and courses.

Second, our methods of teaching thought and action must *require* activity on the part of students. In its simplest definition, critical thinking involves the acquisition and use of information to solve problems and make judgments. These are active processes, and they can be fostered only if learners are required to use them, refine them, and test them. Joan Fulton, a colleague of mine, puts it this way: "When a student watches television, his mind is passive. He does not organize the action of the characters or plot. He doesn't need to reflect on the story, or act on it, to construct the events into a sequence. Why should he consciously consider the situation of the characters, particularly the causes and outcomes of their behavior? The question of 'What happens next?,' which keeps him watching, explains why he is passive. He waits for the story writers to make the relationships for him."

Full, varied, and active experience, in contact with the reality of the world, provides elements for guiding the processes of thinking. The strategies and techniques described in the chapters of this volume emphasize the active involvement of students. In a study of critical thinking in typical classrooms, Smith (1977) found that critical thinking was influenced by students' participation in classroom exchange both among themselves and with the teacher. The activity that is required by independent study can also contribute to the skills and attitudes of practical reason and action. Margaretta Claggett, a senior student on our campus, recently interviewed a dozen teachers about their philosophy of education as independent study. She said about her project that "it was vague and that in itself excited me. I believed that after spending the better part of my life preparing for the future, I was finally being allowed to do something real, something that might mean something to someone someday."

In respect to action, the relationship between thinking and feeling becomes important in learning and teaching. A book on critical thinking may appear to ignore feeling, yet, as Yinger points out, attitudes and dispositions are important to effective thought. This is especially true in the practical realm of thinking and acting on problems of everyday life. Sigel (1977, p. 74) describes it this way:

> Preoccupation with critical functioning, while no doubt critical, is still, I think, a misplaced emphasis. The place of [the] cognitive apparatus is filtering or processing information and relating the outside through the inside to the outside again . . . . At the same time, we are fully aware that [the] information as it is attended to, perceived, processed, reorganized, etc., is influenced by the heat it generates: the excitement, the interest, or the boredom, the fear that it generates or the pleasure. All of these are concomitants and are intimately intertwined with cognition.

The work of William Perry (1970) and others is especially helpful to use here. He suggests that college students move through characteristic stages of response as they judge knowledge and values, proceeding from dualistic and absolute to contextual and realistic. Perry's is a theory of both cognition and emotion and of how they work together toward the development of "commitment." I might call this the ability to act effectively and confidently based on equally effective and confident thought. Perry's ideas have implications for instruction. Teachers can help students to develop effective thought and action. Knefelkamp (1974) and Widick (1975) have used experiential learning approaches coupled with a sufficient amount of structure to move students along in this process of development. Furedy and Furedy (1979) propose a course design which does the same thing.

Perry's ideas raise an important difficulty for efforts to move students to action. Students may not be ready psychologically to commit themselves to the results of their thinking, and even where they already are, thinking can still be a scary business. This is especially true in controversial and emotionally charged areas. "When we speak of 'insight' . . . it is not just seeing something new. It's feeling. And what the person is feeling is both the promise and threat of this unknown that is just opening up. When we think new thoughts, we are really changing our relations with the world around us" (Gruber, 1974, p. 249).

The teaching task is to provide both the *challenging* activities, problems, and questions that stimulate these insights and feelings and the *supporting* structure and personal relationships that allow students to try out these new and maybe troublesome ways of thinking.

To Teachers of Critical Thinking

Success at fostering critical thinking requires a number of ingredients. As individual teachers, we have little control over many of them— student readiness, the resources and commitment of institutions, the reward for learning critical thinking. However, we do have our own assumptions, knowledge, and skills as powerful means to the end of fostering critical thinking. We need to become more skilled. We hope that sourcebooks such as this one and the kind of continuing education that has been suggested in these chapters will help us to do just that. But we also must become increasingly optimistic and confident about our ability to teach students not only the content and methods of our disciplines but how to use them as well. The survival of this society may or may not depend on it, but surely this task can be stimulating and rewarding for students and teachers alike.

References

Anscombe, G. E. M. *Intentions.* Oxford: Blackwell, 1957.

Biber, B. "Thinking and Feeling." Paper presented at annual meeting of the National Association for the Education of Young Children. November 10–13, 1977.

Furedy, J. J., and Furedy, C. "Course Design for Critical Thinking." *Improving College and University Teaching,* 1979, *27* (3), 99–101.

Gruber, H. E. *Darwin on Man: A Psychological Study of Scientific Creativity.* New York: Dutton, 1974.

Knefelkamp, L. L. "Developmental Instruction: Fostering Intellectual and Personal Growth in College Students." Unpublished doctoral dissertation, University of Minnesota, 1974.

Perry, W. G. *Forms of Intellectual and Ethical Development in the College Years.* New York: Holt, Rinehart and Winston, 1970.

Raz, J. (Ed.) *Practical Reasoning.* Oxford: Clarendon Press, 1978.

Schulz, D. E. "The Living Museum." *Change: The Magazine of Learning,* 1980, *12* (1), 10.

Schwab, J. J. *The Practical: A Language for Curriculum.* Washington, D.C.: National Education Association, 1970.

Sigel, I. E. *Cognitive Development from Childhood to Adolescence: A Constructivist Perspective.* New York: Holt, Rinehart and Winston, 1977.

Smith, D. G. "College Classroom Interactions and Critical Thinking." *Journal of Educational Psychology,* 1977, *69* (2), 180–190.

Widick, C. C. "An Evaluation of Developmental Instruction in a University Setting." Unpublished doctoral dissertation, University of Minnesota, 1975.

Robert E. Young, formerly associate director of the Center for Improving Teaching Effectiveness, is now director of the Office of Instructional Development at the University of North Dakota. He is interested in the thinking activities of both students and teachers in higher education. The incentive and idea for this book grew out of work with faculty members as they try to foster critical thinking among an increasingly diverse student body.

Index

E

F

G

H

I

J

K

Y

Z

New Directions Quarterly Sourcebooks

New Directions for Teaching and Learning is one of several distinct series of quarterly sourcebooks published by Jossey-Bass. The sourcebooks in each series are designed to serve both as *convenient compendiums* of the latest knowledge and practical experience on their topics and as *long-life reference tools.*

One-year, four-sourcebook subscriptions for each series cost $18 for individuals (when paid by personal check) and $30 for institutions, libraries, and agencies. Single copies of earlier sourcebooks are available at $6.95 each *prepaid* (or $7.95 each when *billed*).

A complete listing is given below of current and past sourcebooks in the *New Directions for Teaching and Learning* series. The titles and editors-in-chief of the other series are also listed. To subscribe, or to receive further information, write: New Directions Subscriptions, Jossey-Bass Inc., Publishers, 433 California Street, San Francisco, California 94104.

New Directions for Teaching and Learning
Kenneth E. Eble and John Noonan, Editors-in-Chief
1980: 1. *Improving Teaching Styles,* Kenneth E. Eble
2. *Learning, Cognition, and College Teaching,* Wilbert J. McKeachie

New Directions for Child Development
William Damon, Editor-in-Chief

New Directions for College Learning Assistance
Kurt V. Lauridsen, Editor-in-Chief

New Directions for Community Colleges
Arthur M. Cohen, Editor-in-Chief
Florence B. Brawer, Associate Editor

New Directions for Continuing Education
Alan B. Knox, Editor-in-Chief

New Directions for Exceptional Children
James J. Gallagher, Editor-in-Chief

New Directions for Experiential Learning
Pamela J. Tate, Editor-in-Chief
Morris T. Keeton, Consulting Editor

New Directions for Higher Education
JB Lon Hefferlin, Editor-in-Chief

New Directions for Institutional Advancement
A. Westley Rowland, Editor-in-Chief

New Directions for Institutional Research
Marvin W. Peterson, Editor-in-Chief

New Directions for Mental Health Services
H. Richard Lamb, Editor-in-Chief

New Directions for Methodology of Social and Behavioral Science
Donald W. Fiske, Editor-in-Chief

New Directions for Program Evaluation
Scarvia B. Anderson, Editor-in-Chief

New Directions for Student Services
Ursula Delworth and Gary R. Hanson, Editors-in-Chief

New Directions for Testing and Measurement
William B. Schrader, Editor-in-Chief